How to be happy after a divorce

Letting go of the past and emerging from divorce happier and more resilient

[Included bonus material - Letting Go Affirmations]

© Copyright 2023 - All rights reserved. The contents of this book may not be reproduced, duplicated or transmitted without direct written permission from the author. Under no circumstances will any legal responsibility or blame be held against the publisher for any reparation, damages, or monetary loss due to the information herein, either directly or indirectly.

Legal Notice: This book is copyright protected. This is only for personal use. You cannot amend, distribute, sell, use, quote or paraphrase any part or the content within this book without the consent of the author.

Disclaimer Notice: Please note the information contained within this document is for educational and entertainment purposes only. Every attempt has been made to provide accurate, up to date and reliable complete information. No warranties of any kind are expressed or implied. Readers acknowledge that the author is not engaging in the rendering of legal, financial, medical or professional advice. The content of this book has been derived from various sources. Please consult a licensed professional before attempting any techniques outlined in this book. By reading this document, the reader agrees that under no circumstances is the author responsible for any losses, direct or indirect, which are incurred as a result of the use of information contained within this document, including, but not limited to, errors, omissions, or inaccuracies.

Dedication

This book is dedicated to all those women who had their dreams crushed and their future made uncertain by the trauma of divorce. You are not alone, and the pain you feel now and all the feelings you are experiencing now will pass. Your life will change irrevocably but you will be stronger for the experience and free to design a new life, and new future, using your experience and lessons learned.

Hopefully, this book will help you not to lose hope in the future and not to give up on love. Trust your strength and stay who you are, because you are great just the way you are. Do not let divorce make you doubt that. Use the experience of so many other women and emerge from feeling angry, resentful, afraid, and uncertain to being hopeful, strong, resilient, and confident. A bright future is ahead of you, make it to be what you always dreamed of.

Table of Contents

Introduction 1

Chapter 1: It's Okay To Move On 7

Chapter 2: What To Expect 17

Chapter 3: Children Are Getting Divorced Too 27

Chapter 4: It's Not About Who's Right 37

Chapter 5: It's Not A Secret 47

Chapter 6: Developing A New Routine 57

Chapter 7: The Key To Letting Go -What if I still can't let go? 65

Chapter 8: Strengthening Your Defenses 81

Chapter 9: If You Are The One To Initiate Divorce 93

Chapter 10: Learning to be Alone 99

Chapter 11: Designing Your Post-divorce Life 109

Chapter 12: Love Again 119

Conclusion 127

Bonus Material: Letting Go Affirmations 131

Introduction

Did you know that the first thing most women did after their divorce became final was to throw away all the bed sheets and buy new ones? I went for a lot of color and pattern, the things I could not do before, as my husband hated my slightly bohemian tendencies. He was an accountant after all.

It sounds trivial but this act—choosing your own bed sheets—is very symbolic of this new stage of your life: there is the grief of course, and the sense of failure, and the fear of the future, but there is also a sense of elation at the freedom you gained. There is so much you can do now that you could not do before.

You do not have to compromise endlessly, or give up on things you wanted because your spouse did not agree with them. You can completely redesign your home. You can eat tofu if you want and give up meat, which was impossible with a man in the house. You can wake up in the middle of the night and watch rom-coms while eating Rocky Road ice cream. Or move that sofa to another spot. Or go back to school! Anything is possible.

Don't be ashamed of this feeling of being finally free. Even if the divorce was not something you wanted, you got the freedom, like it or not. Now it is up to you to decide what to do with it.

Divorce is considered one of the most traumatic experiences in human life. And it is still traumatic even if you desperately wanted that divorce. It affects every aspect of your life. It affects you emotionally, financially, physically, socially, and mentally. You have to adjust all these aspects of your life to the new reality.

How you go through divorce very much depends on the kind of person you are. Are you confident, resilient, and brave? Have you been through a lot already? Did you have to carry most of the burden in your marriage all alone? Did you feel lonely while married? Did you come out of the divorce angry, sad, devastated, lost, relieved, liberated, free, or a combination of all of them?

Divorce means change. Good or bad, like it or not, the change is coming and you will have to deal with it. You might be tempted to try to continue your life as it was before, but it will just postpone the inevitable: the realization that your life will never be the same. Scary for sure.

Even if your marriage was bad, it defined your life. You were a wife. Your lifestyle was defined by you being a part of a couple. Your social life was organized as a part of a couple. Most of your friends were friends to both you and your husband. Your home was organized for married life. You thought that it was forever. You thought you would grow old together and raise grandchildren together. All that is now shaken to the foundations.

Whatever your state of mind and your personality, divorce is one experience you should not go through alone. Not because you are not able to, but because you need to be surrounded by people who love you and who will support you while you are going through all the inevitable stages of grief divorce brings.

And that is what you need right after the divorce: love. Love is the most important thing you lost after your marriage failed, even if you do not remember when you last felt love for the man you were married to. Because most of us get married for love. Love keeps us married, even when it is love for our kids and our need to protect them. And when a marriage fails, you cannot avoid thinking: Did he ever love me? Why does he not love me anymore? What is wrong with me? What could I have done better?

So, get as much love as you can, from friends, family, kids, movies, songs, clubs, and nature. Let yourself cry for the loss of love, let the poison of the lost love and lost dreams of forever-love pour out of you with your tears. And when you are done, and you will be done at some point, pull yourself together and make a plan for the rest of your life. Because you are now free to make it any way you want. And you want to be happy again.

This book will guide you through the process of recovery from the feeling of loss to the feeling of endless possibilities ahead of you.

Together, we will discuss the stages of grief you will be going through (or are already going through). How to recognize them, how to cope with them, and how to get out of them. The book will share with you the wisdom of others who went through the same process, and who made it to the other end stronger and determined to make this new stage of their lives better and happier.

We will talk about how to take care of yourself, since you have probably forgotten how while playing the role of a wife. We will share advice on how to help kids go through the divorce and to understand what is happening. The book will show you the tricks and tips others used to turn grief and sadness into a feeling of optimism and hope.

You might not feel it now, but what is ahead of you is the new, better phase of your life. The phase which will benefit from your experience, and divorce is an experience you can learn a lot from.

We will discuss what you did wrong, what you did right, and how to avoid becoming bitter and hateful towards men; how to love again, how to demand respect, and attention; how to regain your independence, redefine your future and create new dreams in place of the old ones that are gone.

It is hard, and all women who have been through divorce know it. Divorce hurts on a fundamental level. You might get scars, but look at them as your battle scars and carry them with pride. The pain you feel now will fade. Let yourself cry but not too long. Feeling self-pity is not helping. You are better than that. Do not allow your friends and family to smother you with their pity and *understanding*. They do it out of love, but you have a job to do—to rebuild your life from the foundations. Let's do it together.

Chapter 1

It's Okay To Move On

Dona learned that life as she knew it was finished over a bottle of good Merlot. She knew something was off when her husband of ten years invited her to a fancy restaurant for dinner. A truly rare occurrence, but she was happy for small mercies in her sad marriage. Then, after finishing his filet mignon, her husband told her that he wanted a divorce. What? How? Why? She was too shocked to ask any of those questions. All she could think was: What am I going to do now?

Like so many women, Dona immersed herself in her marriage by becoming the best wife she could be. She neglected her friends because now she and her husband had 'their' friends. She dropped out of university, too busy being a wife and a mother. She was fine with making those 'small' sacrifices because they were building their forever life. They had plans for their old age, vacations to exotic places when the kids got older, a cottage by the lake for the family holidays.

All that came crashing down. Everything she knew was gone with those few words: I want a divorce.

Things got worse after that. She had to tell the kids that their dad will not live with them anymore. She had to learn to live on a modest alimony, and sleep in a king-size bed all alone. She kept through her routines because she could not think of what else to do; too shocked to even think about some different life she could build now.

Her friend, Lisa, shook her out of her stupor. She was one of the few friends Dona had from her 'previous life.' She took her to a spa and forced her to spend a day being pampered and drinking champagne. Then she told her to stop griping and count her blessings. Blessings? Being alone in her middle age? "Blessings," said Lisa. "You are finally free to go back to being yourself."

Who am I?

And here we come to one of the many blessings in the painful, devastating state of being a divorced woman. Like so many of us, Dona forgot who she really was. She adapted to her married life and that meant ignoring many parts of her personality that 'did not fit.' She could not even remember what her dreams were before getting married. She loved being married. She loved being cherished and taken care of and doing everything with the love of her life.

At least in the beginning.

Until there was not much cherishing going on and her husband was too busy to do anything with her. Especially things she wanted to do, such as taking the kids to the zoo or going to a museum.

Hopefully, you have a friend like Lisa who will remind you that there is life after the divorce. Very likely a much better life than the one you had.

Start by looking at yourself in the mirror. Not at the wrinkles and sun spots. At you, deep down, at your core. Who are you? Being married or divorced does not define you. Are you deep down adventurous? Curious? Artistic? Athletic? Handy? What did you like doing before you got married? You were studying to be an architect when the marriage derailed your plans. Yes, derailed. Being married is not a personality trait, although so many women take it as such, at great cost to their personality.

It might take some time, but eventually, you will start getting a seed of excitement at the possibilities.

If you recover much faster from your divorce than you and everyone else expected, do not feel guilty. We women always find a reason to feel guilty about something. Living life to the fullest is not a betrayal of your past. It is you spreading your wings, finally.

It is over

The most difficult part of accepting the divorce is that it is so final. Life as you knew it is over. Everything you knew about how to live is now gone. Accept it. It is real. Painful but real and final. It makes you feel so empty and aimless. What you need to do is fill that emptiness with new beginnings.

Hard? You bet. You do not know how to balance a checkbook. You do not know where the breaker box is. How do you turn the lawn mower on? Big deal. Any decent neighbor will help you with all that. And your dad and your brother and your friends. You are not alone. You have people who love you, those who did not promise 'to love you and cherish you until death do you part" and then bail. Those who love you for who you are. You can count on them; they are there for you.

Best friends' intervention

You probably feel awful about horribly neglecting so many good friends you had before you got married. You were so immersed in your marriage that they somehow did not fit into your new life. You forgot their birthdays and ignored their divorces and job losses. And now they are here for you when you need them.

Chapter 1

Learn from it. You messed up, but now you can make it up to them.

They are probably the only friends you now have since so many people you thought were friends were actually your husband's friends and dropped you like a hot potato now that you are not with him anymore.

Some of them might be afraid that, now that you are single, their husbands might pay you attention. Others do not find you appropriate for their social circle now that you are a 'divorcee.' You also do not have much money anymore. Some friends. Good riddance.

Channel that anger

Anger is a common feeling after a divorce. Sometimes because there is a new woman involved, or the divorce came out of the blue when you thought that everything in the marriage looked idyllic. Or because your ex did what you wanted to do for such a long time but did not have the guts.

You want to punch him in the face to take out that smug expression you hate so much. Since that is illegal and the kids would not like it, you need to find a channel for all that rage. How about kickboxing? Or a self-defense course? Or even tennis or volleyball or anything that will make you sweat and drain all that aggression.

Being physically active is one of the best things you can do for yourself immediately after the divorce. It will make you feel better with all that endorphin flooding your system. It will make you get out of bed when all you want to do is wallow in self-pity.

And it will make you drop some pounds and tighten your butt, so you can buy some nice new clothes.

The heartbreak diet

Don't be surprised if you start losing weight after the divorce. It happens to most women. There is an official name for it: the heartbreak diet. To some extent, it is all the stress. You just do not feel for food. In part, it is anger management—the physical activities you engage in instead of punching your ex. One reason is healthy and the other is not.

Stress is an expected result of a divorce. Everything you knew about your life is being shaken and stirred. Even all that ice cream you are consuming in the dark moments of despair is not helping. You might like seeing all those pounds dropping, but not if it means your health is affected. There is a reason why it is called 'a heartbreak diet.'

The research shows that stress is not only a state of mind. It physically affects your body. It can cause a range of physical issues you really do not need in the middle of dealing with a divorce. You need to take care of yourself.

If you have kids, they are probably the only reason you are getting out of bed in the morning while you are still in the deepest throes of divorce despair. You need to be there for them, so be there for yourself too. Fill the fridge with healthy goodies and make some delicious meals. Cooking is very therapeutic. Make things your ex did not like, such as smoothies and salads and quiches. Indulge the kids with fruit tarts and banana pancakes. Good health is your first line of defense. Take care of it.

If you are losing weight while eating well and getting all the exercise you can stand, enjoy it. It happens to so many women. Could it be because looking good makes you feel more confident, more positive, and even more desirable? Good for you. Imagine the feeling if you can fit in your daughter's jeans?

Depression blues

According to the Holmes-Rahe Life Stress Inventory, divorce is one of the five most stressful events in human life, second only after the death of a loved one. Other causes are moving, major injury or illness, and job loss. While all women suffer from such devastating changes in their lives, some fall into a deep depression.

The symptoms of depression look very much like what you would expect when you have freshly learned that life as you know is over:

- Sadness;
- Hopelessness;
- Loss of interest in anything you cared for before;
- Feeling overwhelmed;
- Unable to focus;
- Crying at the drop of a hat;
- Difficulty sleeping;
- Sleeping too much;
- Eating too much or not at all; and
- Contemplating suicide.

If all or some of these symptoms persist for more than a few weeks, they are signs of depression and they may mean you need help from a professional. There is no shame in seeking help when you need it. If depression is not treated, it can become a chronic disease and disrupt your life long-term. You have enough to deal with without it.

There is no rule about how long you will feel miserable after your divorce papers have been signed. You might feel like you are finally back to your normal self and then something will trigger a memory and you will fall apart. It is normal. Give yourself a break. Have a cry, take a day off from work, go for a walk or just hide in the bathroom and breathe deeply for a few minutes. Whatever works for you.

The five stages of divorce grief

The stages we go through when suffering any grief were first defined in 1969 by Elisabeth Kübler-Ross in her book *On Death and Dying*. While the stages were defined as something we feel after losing a loved one, they surprisingly follow the stages we go through after suffering any grief.

The stages are not linear. They do not go in the same order for everyone. Some of us skip some stages. But it is important to learn what you might expect, and what will probably come next. It helps to know that you are going through a process that will eventually end.

Denial

Denial means refusing to accept what has happened. It also means feeling overwhelmed and feeling like life has become meaningless. You feel the shock and numbness as your body and mind can only deal with as much emotion as you can handle. Eventually, this shock fades and the so-far suppressed feelings start to surface.

Anger

Anger is often the first feeling we start to sense after the denial fades away. You might not be exactly sure what the target of your anger is: your ex, yourself, life's unfairness, your mother-in-law, anything, and anyone. This powerful anger is an indication of the strong feelings you had about your ex and the life you had together.

Bargaining

Your first instinct is to want your life to go back to the way it was. "What if..." is the most common thought. If you had done this or that, things would have been different. Trying to turn back time, to pretend that it did not happen, they are all just your attempts to avoid accepting the inevitable. Remaining in the past, you try to avoid feeling some of the hurt—at least temporarily.

Depression

The bargaining phase looks to the past. Depression is about the present. As anger fades and bargaining does not work, depression sets in and it feels like the pain will never end. It is ok to feel depressed for a while. It is an integral part of healing.

Acceptance

Acceptance does not mean that you are OK with what happened and that you are suddenly feeling fine. It just means that you now accept this new reality and accept that this is what you have to live with now. It does not mean that you are now finished with grieving or ready to move on. It is just one more stage in the grieving process on the way to healing.

Acknowledging different stages of grief and accepting that they are all important parts of healing is very important. The worst you can do after your marriage ends is to pretend that life goes on as before and that you are fine. Suppressing strong feelings will eat you from the inside. You have to deal with it so that you can move on.

And moving on you will. We will discuss the tools you need for this battle you have ahead of you. Or you can see it as an adventure. And like for any adventure, you will need the right tools, the right equipment, the right shoes and, most importantly, the right attitude. In the next chapters, we will offer you all you need. Except for the shoes.

Chapter 2

What To Expect

Remember when your mom (or dad or grandma) died how devastated you were? All you wanted to do was curl up in your bed and cry. But you could not because there were all those things to take care of: arrange the funeral, chose a casket, clothes to bury her in, write an obituary, prepare the memorial service, contact the insurance company, mom's lawyer...

Divorce is very much like that. Endless papers, meetings, and responsibilities you have to deal with because your entire future depends on doing them right. You do not feel capable of dealing with all that. Your head feels woozy and your mind is still reeling from the enormity of changes that are coming. You have enough on your plate just dealing with your emotions, practical things seem beyond you.

There are surely people in your family who are willing to help, but it is important that you find the strength to get fully involved in all the formality that comes with the dissolving (death?) of your marriage. For many reasons, but most importantly to start grabbing the steering wheel of your life. Because, as of now, you are in the driving seat.

If you were lucky and smart to get a good divorce lawyer, he or she prepared you for what to expect and gave you a list of things to take care of.

In any case, make a list of things you think should be done and show it to someone in your family to make sure you did not miss anything.

Paperwork

Hate it as much as you want, paperwork is the way of things in our modern life. You need a copy of your divorce papers for any future contracts and transactions you will be doing, from signing lease papers to opening a bank account. You do not have to read it if it makes you sad or mad. Just get a copy and keep it in a safe place. Scan it and save a copy. Actually, make many copies, you will need them all the time.

If you do not want to keep your married name (some women want to because of the kids), you have to change all your personal documents that have your married name: driving license, health insurance papers, passport and any other documents and licenses you have. That will be the first instance you will need to show your divorce papers.

Go to your bank (with a copy of your divorce papers) and close your joint accounts. Keep only accounts your ex has no access to, in your personal name (after you change it). Very likely, the division of assets has been arranged during the divorce proceedings, but the sooner it is all clear and finished, the better. You will also have a clearer picture of how much money you have to work with.

Look at your credit cards and cancel all cards that are joint with your ex. Actually, get rid of most credit cards except one or two. You will most likely not have the same amount of money to spend as before. Credit cards are so tempting after the divorce. Forget retail therapy, it will cost you later when the bills come.

Money

Money is often the biggest bone of contention during divorce proceedings and the biggest reason people who loved each other once start a bitter war that ends in the total breakdown of civilities. Don't do it. Let the lawyer fight for you. You are emotionally vulnerable, you are not thinking straight, and you do not need the additional pain.

Unless there was a large amount of money involved, most women get out of their marriage with much less money than they had before. Even if you have your own salary, you are now working with one income only, which has to be enough for all your, and your kids', needs.

In most families, the husband is the one to take care of bills and paperwork. It is now your job. Go through the checkbook and bills and find out what bills have to be paid, monthly, yearly, or at any interval.

Hopefully, your lawyer arranged with the lawyer of your ex that the children's support money is to be deposited regularly to your account. Make sure your lawyer has your account number if it is a new one. The same goes for the payment of kids' school tuition and other expenses, as well as alimony if there is one.

If you have to talk to your ex about such matters, make sure you are in the right frame of mind for such a conversation. If there is a disagreement, do not explode, just tell him that your lawyer will get in touch. Or that you will talk again when he has taken care of things he is supposed to. Or when he is more reasonable. It is better to do these things over the phone so you can end it before it escalates.

Write to the kids' school and inform the principal and their teacher about the divorce. It is important that the school knows that the kids are going through tough times and to allow them some slack.

Will

You must have seen it in the movies, but it happens, in reality, more often than you believe: people get divorced and forget to change their will. So, if something happens to you, the ex gets all the money.

Even if there is not much money, make sure that your will reflects how you feel right now about the distribution of your assets. Young or old, none of us knows how much time we have left on this earth.

If you have an insurance policy, review it and make the necessary changes to adjust to the new situation.

Passwords

It is common for spouses to know each other's passwords for email and social media accounts. Change all that. Even if you parted amicably, you do not want to give him the chance to spy on your messages or browsing history.

Change passwords for any online banking or shopping accounts you still have opened.

Give yourself time to breathe

Taking care of all these formalities is exhausting. But, dealing with all that will also give you a sense of regaining control of your life. That does not mean that you have to do it all at once, or that you have to do it alone.

If you have an accountant or a lawyer in the family, let him or her help and teach you what you need to know so you can do it alone in the future.

While you are busy putting your life in order, you might be so busy you forget to eat or breathe or rest or exercise. In other words, you might pretend that everything is all under control and that you've got it. You do, but you are still grieving. Take care of yourself.

This is where friends come in. There is no reason that dealing with banking cannot be combined with lunch at your favorite Italian restaurant with your best friends. Or that dealing with the condo administration in your condo building cannot be combined with a visit to your hairdresser.

Get a personal trainer

You might be more comfortable getting a personal trainer than a therapist, but during this stage, their role is very similar: to support you and help you deal with all the changes you are going through.

Getting a gym membership is not enough, it is easy to find an excuse not to go. Getting a personal trainer means being involved with a person who will explain to you why you need to take care of your physical well-being so you can survive this difficult period of your life more or less sane.

It might sound like a luxury when you are trying to cut expenses, but a personal trainer is someone who will help you take care of your health and nutrition, and if you are lucky, will offer words of support when dealing with emotional issues. Many women develop strong bonds and friendships with their personal trainers.

When to look for a therapist

You are now intimately familiar with all the signs of grief. You know that your crying bouts are normal and that you need to let yourself go through all the stages of grief so you can get out of it mentally healthy. But, there are times when you cannot deal with all of that on your own.

If you feel depressed for more than a few weeks, you need to talk to a therapist. Often, all you need is just a talk, to ensure that what you are going through is a part of the process. At times, you need some medication, or to join a support group. Your therapist will be able to advise you.

There is no more stigma about seeing a therapist. They take care of your mental health just like physicians take care of your physical health. And the end of your marriage is the time when your mind needs more help than your body.

Joining a support group might help if you feel like talking to other people who are going through the same things you are. You might find it helpful to see that you are not the biggest mess of all. Other people find it depressing. Try it and see how you feel. Your physician can recommend a group in your neighborhood. Your friends probably also know about some.

Find a funny side

Did you wonder how we find it hilarious to watch people go nuts while getting a divorce in the movies, but the same things are not so funny when happening to us? Well, maybe they are funny if you decide to look at the funny side. Hopefully, you have that one friend who is always ready to laugh at just about anything. That is the kind of person you need now.

Instead of despairing, try to laugh about the idiocy of so many things that are happening. Sharing assets? Perfect opportunity for some hilarity. Fighting over wedding gifts? Or giant TV?

Have sleepover parties with your friends and trash your ex with them over a lot of wine and chocolate. Watch rom-coms together and compare the characters in the movie to your ex or yourself. If you make up your mind, you can find a funny side to things that looked grim before.

Keep track of your progress

Writing a daily entry in your journal can be very therapeutic. You can put on paper everything you have done, how you felt, what you said and what you did not; what affected you and what did not.

Even more important is to go back through your journal from time to time and see your progress. You might feel like you are dragging your feet or that you are still drowning in sorrow and grief, but reading your journal can show you the steady progress and slow but sure recovery.

Small steps

When you start feeling better, you might be tempted to start making plans for some big changes in your life. Do not rush. Your emotions are still in turmoil, you are hurt and out of balance. There will be time for big changes, but first, get yourself back in shape, physically and emotionally. Take long walks, read good books, and meet friends and favorite family members. Spend time with the kids. Take it easy and slowly. Spend time getting time to know yourself again, now that you are getting out of the marriage cocoon and becoming a butterfly.

How to know when you are ready for the new phase of your life?

Some scientists say that it takes about 18 months to recover from divorce. Others are more honest and say that they do not know because divorces are messy and every person is different. It all depends on whether you wanted a divorce or not. Some women have been preparing for it for months or even years and it came as a welcome relief. Others refuse to accept the loss of their previous life and are resistant to the inevitable changes.

In most cases, your recovery will come slowly but surely and one day, sometimes suddenly, you will feel a sense of relief. The pain will be replaced with a sense of freedom and anticipation. You will stop thinking about the past and start thinking about the future.

You can help this process by deliberately cutting ties with everything that keeps you linked to the past. Stop calling your ex, stop thinking about the vacations you used to have together, and stop reliving the past, even the good parts. At least for the time being, until you firmly establish your new reality.

And one day you will be watching some romantic movie and start thinking about dating. How nice it would be to meet someone new and exciting. Or you will dig through your stuff and find your paints and remember how much you enjoyed painting. Or dancing. Or studying. And life will start looking bright and you will feel in balance and all will be good with the world. You will be ready to start the new, exciting period of your life. But we will talk more about that in the next chapters.

Chapter 3

CHILDREN ARE GETTING DIVORCED TOO

If you are a mother, nothing is more important during the separation and divorce than being there for your child or children. You become a mama bear, there to protect your cubs. You know that you have to put on hold your own feelings and explain to the kids what is going on. All without going into any gory details.

Divorce can have devastating effects on children. It may cause their withdrawal from their friends; they might have attachment issues and a range of behavioral problems. Divorce can make some children depressed, and cause deep anxiety and the effects may last long into their adulthood.

Depending on their age, most children are aware that things are not well between their parents. They might witness fights and screaming matches. Even when parents behave civilly towards each other, children know when things are not right. If there is another woman in their father's life, they probably figured it out long before you.

It is crucial to talk to the children as soon as the atmosphere in their home changes and there is a big chance of separation and divorce. Encourage them to talk and ask questions. Explain just how complicated relationships between adults can be and that the problems between the parents are never the kids' fault.

If their father moves out of the home, ideally, both parents should sit with the children and talk to them about how much they love them even if they do not all live together anymore.

The strongest effects of divorce on children can be expected during the first year. It is important that you know what to expect and how to react.

Anger

Anger is one of the most common reactions of kids to their parents' divorce. Their whole life is shattered. Their sense of security is lost. The parents are their whole world. They expect parents to take care of them, keep them safe, and provide for their needs. If divorced, children feel like their parents will not be able to fulfill that role.

The effects are particularly strong if the divorce is accompanied by conflict and fights between the parents. They respond with anger as that is what they feel coming from their parents. Their anger is not always focused and they might express their strong emotions by starting fights with their siblings or schoolmates. They also might act up against a parent they blame for the divorce, whether it is true or not.

Withdrawal

Some children are affected by divorce and respond by withdrawing socially. They refuse to talk to their parents, avoid their friends, and refuse to participate in their social activities, sports, or hobbies. They often feel shame or guilt, believing that they somehow contributed to the divorce, especially if they had been having behavioral issues. They think that their father would not move out if they were not so naughty or acting out.

Children may also refuse to meet with their friends because they are afraid of questions they might be asked and not know how to answer them.

Problems in School

Divorce can take kids' minds off their responsibilities in school and they can be so emotionally distraught that school feels like too much to deal with and unimportant in the grand scheme of things. They start skipping school, not doing their homework, or just losing interest and focus.

As parents are involved in their struggle, they often neglect to participate in children's activities or to pay attention to their school responsibilities. Kids take advantage of this lack of attention to skip school.

When separation and divorce are amicable and both parents are determined to help children go through this tough period, the effect of divorce on children is much less difficult.

Relationship Problems

During the divorce, one or both parents become unavailable to children, making them feel like their support system is collapsing and they have nobody they can count on. They start having a problem with other relationships, such as with other adults, teachers, friends, and relatives. Very young children might turn to other adults for attention and affection and sometimes form a clingy and unhealthy attachment to other adults that are in their lives, such as teachers, nannies, or babysitters.

Acting out

During such emotionally charged period of their lives such as divorce, it is expected for children to act out one way or another. Temper tantrums, fighting, stubbornness, disobedience, and aggression are all to be expected, especially if the divorce is full of conflict and intense emotions.

On one hand, such behavior is the result of children not knowing how to channel their unresolved and poorly understood emotions and the feeling of insecurity, and on the other hand, their wish to punish their parents for disrupting their lives. The more conflict they observe between their parents during the divorce, the worse the children act out.

Sleeping and eating problems

Divorce commonly disrupts children's normal routine, causing them to skip meals, go to sleep too late, or sleep too long in the morning. Parents might neglect to take care of kids' routines while being emotionally distraught, or the children react to the strong emotions that charge their home during that period.

It gets worse once parents live in separate households and they have to spend part of their time with each parent and adapt to different routines. This might affect their regular diet and the lack of sufficient sleep might affect their ability to perform in school. The anxiety, a permanent company during this period of their lives, also affects the kids' appetite and ability to have sufficient and uninterrupted sleep.

Risky Behavior

One way of acting out during the divorce is to engage in risky behavior. Children, particularly teens and adolescents, attempt shoplifting, smoking, drinking alcohol, and having unsafe sex. This can be the need for instant gratification, an attempt to avoid dealing with their real emotions, or the way of punishing parents for what they did to their lives, feeling that the parents do not really care for them and how they feel.

Poor health

The lack of parental attention, the disruption of the normal routine, the lack of normal nutrition, anxiety, or depression can affect kids' physical health. They can start complaining of upset stomach, headaches, or unspecified pain. The complaints can also be the attempt to get attention from parents if they are not getting enough during this period.

Guilt

Children often feel that the divorce is somehow their fault. They think of all the 'bad' things they have done and believe that if they were not naughty their parents would still be together. This feeling persists even when parents assure them that the divorce is by no means their fault.

Children often try to show parents that they can be good by displaying excessively nice behavior, trying to please parents in any way they know how, hoping that it would make them change their minds and stay together.

Developmental issues

Some children, especially younger ones, react to the divorce by regressing in their development, i.e., wetting the bed or sucking their thumb. This may be their attempt to self-soothe lacking emotional support from their parents. It can also be a sign of anxiety and depression.

The right things to do

If you think you are devastated by the divorce, just imagine how the kids feel. You are an adult and know what to expect. You know that you will be able to deal with it all, even if at the moment you feel like your world is falling apart. But all the kids know is that two people who are their whole world are fighting and that they will not be together anymore to take care of them. They do not know what it means. You need to help them understand what is going on and what it means for them.

If possible, start by talking to the kids together with your ex. Explain to the kids that their parents both love them and that nothing will change that, even when the parents do not live together anymore. If they do not want to talk, if they are hostile and angry, let them be. Tell them that you are there for them whenever they want to talk and will answer any question they have.

Find an ambassador

While you are talking to them, kids might lash out and tell you that they hate you or that they know you do not love them or you would never get a divorce. They might insult you and be very rude. Do not lose your patience with them, but behave just like you always behaved when they were rude and do not put up with it. Insist on civil, polite behavior. They will feel comforted to see you behaving normally.

The kids' feelings are all over the place. Try to find an opportunity when they are calmer to talk to them. It might even be good to ask your parents or some relative or friend to talk to them if they are close to them. They might blame you for what happened, so a neutral person might be someone they will listen to. Just make sure that the kids know that you are there for them any time they want to talk.

No blame game

Make sure that the kids are not pawns in your fight with your spouse. Do not use them for sending messages or for spying on your ex. Kids need to understand that what happened between you and your ex is in no way their fault.

While you have to explain why the divorce happened, make sure not to blame your ex. It is enough for kids to understand that there are times when adults are having irreconcilable differences and that it is better for everyone involved if they are separated. The kids might disagree with you, but remind them that the fighting they probably heard is not a pleasant way to live. Separate, both their parents can have good, peaceful life the kids will be a part of.

Take care of your and their mental health

Controlling your anger and resentment and finding a way to be calm will help them to feel the same. They are watching you and unconsciously reflecting your mood and behavior. Spend time in nature and invite them to join you. Take them to the gym with you. Watch funny movies together. Teach them how to meditate and how to control their anger with deep breathing.

Kids need both parents

If your ex agrees to manage boundaries and set rules for the kids with you, they will have a much easier time adjusting to the new reality. They might enjoy parents trying to outdo each other with presents and bribing them out of guilt, but it does not work long term.

Kids need routine and stability. During a turmoil such as a divorce, anything you can do to help them deal with it will benefit them long term. Research shows that the kids whose parents worked together on co-parenting after the divorce recover from this period much faster and with very few emotional scars.

Remember that you taking care of yourself during this period will ultimately benefit the kids. They really do not need a mom who is spending all her time in bed crying and cursing her ex, even if that is all you want to do. That would scare them out of their wits. They would feel like they have to take care of you. That is more than they should have to bear.

If you are really in a bad place, you might want to send the kids to their grandparents' or some other saner environment. And be honest with yourself, for the sake of the kids: if you need help from a therapist, get it. Otherwise, the kids will need it too.

Children who are lovingly supported during a divorce recover much faster and are more likely to accept divorce as a better of two evils—a better alternative to an unhappy life with two parents. The loving behavior of both parents might help kids avoid potential bitterness and lack of trust in the institution of marriage or the opposite sex.

Healthy self-interest

Kids by nature are self-centered little things. If you give them what they need, they will recover from the divorce much faster than you. They need to feel loved, secure and safe. They dread not knowing what is coming and what to expect, but once they see that the divorce is not affecting them in any major way, except that they will see their parents at different times, they will accept it.

Kids are often angry if their economic circumstances change after the divorce. If mom has to move to a smaller house or apartment or if there is no more money for camps and vacations and expensive gadgets, they might blame their parents for that. They might blame mom for making dad leave or blame dad for leaving them.

It is up to you to show them that they should not allow material things to define their lives. They are better than that. And they can always get small jobs such as taking a paper route, mowing a neighbor's lawn, or babysitting if they really need that new computer game.

Chapter 4

It's Not About Who's Right

Bashing your ex immediately after he told you the dreaded words, "I want a divorce," is a popular and satisfying pastime, especially with your friends who went through it themselves. It is his fault that your marriage is over, that you are miserable, that you have no idea what the future holds... OK, indulge in it for a while, but not too long. Because it is useless and unproductive. It changes nothing and it solves nothing.

Who is at fault?

Being angry when facing a divorce is normal, especially if you did not see it coming. You need someone to blame for the failure of your marriage and for the drastic changes you are facing. And your ex is handy. You also might blame yourself, your lawyer, your mother-in-law, or his secretary/dental hygienist/masseuse.

Finding who to blame is only useful from the legal point and your lawyer suggests it. Your lawyer will know what types of divorces exist in your state or your country and will suggest the type that is the most appropriate and most beneficial for you.

At times, the reason for the divorce is your husband's alcoholism, philandering, mental or physical abuse, or some other legally defined reason. In that case, your lawyer will suggest that the at-fault type of divorce will provide you better outcome financially, or full custody of the children. You have the legal right to blame him, the creep. But it is more beneficial to let the lawyer work on that blame and you do not dwell on it. Because it will poison you.

Most divorces are legally defined as no-fault. It means two people who loved each other and married each other came to the point that they are not happy in that marriage anymore. So divorce is the way for them to be happier in the future. Sounds logical, right? If so, why do you feel so angry and want to bash his face in? Because it is easier than looking in the mirror.

Look at the roots

When you finally stop wasting time being angry and honestly look at your marriage, you will see that there were red flags for a long time. But you ignored them because you wanted to stay married. Or you felt you deserved to be bullied or abused, that you did not know how to set healthy boundaries, that you never learned to stand up for yourself because you wanted the kids to have both parents, etc. etc.

There were surely times when you thought about the divorce. What would it mean, and what would your life look like? And you did not like the changes you see happening, even if the changes were for the better.

So when your husband initiates the divorce, you are angry at him and yourself for ignoring the signs and being afraid to act on them.

Moving from the past

Holding on to your anger and continuing to blame your ex for the end of your marriage is useless on so many levels, but most importantly, because it is keeping you in the past. The past that is now over and done with. You can move on only when you stop the blaming game and accept that what is done is done. What if and if only are useless and change nothing.

The only good thing that can come from endlessly analyzing what happened and how it came to this point is as a way to learn from your mistakes. Yes, your mistakes. Because if you do not learn from what happened, you are most likely to make the same mistakes again. What mistakes, you might be wondering. There is a whole list, and you better look at it carefully:

- You allow him to be rude and disrespectful to you without sitting down with him and telling him that it is not acceptable;
- You let him deal with all financial matters because it was easier, and never know where the money went and how much money there was to work with;
- You ignored your friends because he did not like them;
- You did all the parenting, and did not put your foot down when he never went to the kids' football games or piano recitals;
- You pretended that it was OK when he stayed at work late day after day;
- He never wanted to do anything with you and you accepted it;
- When you complained about his behavior, he called you a nag and you so got used to it that you started to believe him.

This is just to start you off thinking about this and being honest with yourself. When you open up yourself to seriously thinking about your marriage and the real reason why it ended, you will find out that there are many red flags that should have told you that your marriage was not healthy and not worth holding on to, for any reason.

Do not accept the role of a victim

By blaming your ex for the end of the marriage or for all the bad things you had to suffer during the marriage, you put yourself in the role of a victim. Do you really like that role? Aren't you a strong, independent, self-confident woman? Playing a victim allows you endless self-pity that will keep you in that role forever, effectively preventing you from healing from the divorce and moving on.

Learning to forgive

Even if your ex was an abusive, cruel, self-centered, narcissistic ass, and you are fully entitled to hating his guts, holding on to your anger and blame will not help you heal from the past. Forgiveness is not about him; it is about you.

Holding on to the memories of all harm that your ex has done, including ending your marriage, keeps you in an endless loop of negative feelings that so fill you with pain that there is no space for healing and hope.

Forgiving does not mean forgetting. It means consciously deciding to move on, to forgive your ex for the hurt he has caused you, drawing the line under that period of your life and starting from scratch. With the knowledge and experience that will keep you safe from the same type of hurt in the future.

Holding on to the grudge and negative feelings might color all your future relationships. It might help you recognize red flags and refuse to be drawn into the lies and double-faced behavior, but it will not make you paint all men with the same brush.

Until you can forgive your ex for the hurt he has caused you, he will have power over how you feel. Forgiveness releases you and frees you from being influenced by him even after the divorce and after being free from his behavior.

The power of empathy

To be able to forgive your ex requires a great dose of empathy. It asks you to try to understand his motivation, the roots of his behavior and what his behavior is doing to his happiness and his well-being. Not yours, his. Because that is the man you loved once and you were happy with for a time. For years, maybe.

You should have it in you to try to see what is happening from his point of view and accept it, even if you do not agree with it. Your empathy will release you from the feeling of hate or resentment and make you free to feel hope for the future.

Kids need both parents

Holding on to your grudge and bashing your ex for months and years is bad for you but it is devastating for your children. Children usually love both parents and do not like when one of them is being insulted, blamed, and accused of being evil or bad. They particularly do not like learning all sorts of sordid details about what he has done and with whom.

Let children have their love for their father. Protect them if he is truly evil, but that is rare. If he is mean and self-centered, let them figure it out on their own. They will.

Whether you like it or not, unless he is found unfit to be a father for any reason, your husband will be your children's father forever. He is going to be part of your life and you better make it as bearable as possible. Civil behavior and resisting calling him names in front of the kids is a good start.

It is not unusual for children to take sides in the divorce and blame one parent or another for the interruption of their normal life. Commonly, they feel for their mother for being left alone to raise them and feel angry at their father if he left you for another woman. But if you keep bashing him in front of them, it might backfire and they might resent you for it.

Dona's story

Dona married very young and had her son when she was 22. Her marriage to her son's father lasted only two years. Being married to an alcoholic prone to violent outbursts when drunk did not make her life easy and the divorce was a relief.

Everyone told her that her son needed his father, even a drunk one, so she facilitated their regular meetings and allowed her son to spend some time with his father, even if she was dreading what might be happening during such time. Fortunately, her ex's parents were involved in their time together and their love and care made that time pleasant and safe for the child.

As Dona's son grew, he was less and less interested in meeting his father and at one point told his mom that he did not want to see him anymore. When she asked why, he told her that his dad often took him to a bar or took him to meet his friends while they were drinking together. He found his father unpleasant and boring and refused to see him anymore.

Dona always wondered if she did her son a disservice for allowing him to spend time with his father and possibly allowing him to provide a bad influence. But she trusted that her son had enough guidance from the love and stability she provided in her home that he would be able to see his father for what he was when he was old enough.

If you persist in this blame game for a prolonged period of time, you are creating a bad, negative atmosphere in your home that children hate. Do not be surprised if they start preferring to spend time with their father instead of you. Who wants to listen to endless griping and complaining? If you want to heal from the divorce and move on with your life, children want it even more.

There is a good chance that your ex will try to bribe the children with expensive gifts to 'be on his side.' Do not try to out-bribe him. Let the kids enjoy presents and never try to tell them that it is just a bribe. A pleasant atmosphere, regular routine, and stability are far more important for them and your ex cannot compete with that. Try to joke about it and tell the kids how nice it is of their dad to buy them such nice gifts so you do not have to do it.

It is a process

Do not expect yourself to be all reasonable and forgiving right away. Acknowledge your feelings of hurt; scream, yell and curse (away from the kids) if you need to, get it out of your system and then drop it. Let yourself move on, let go of the feeling of hurt and the need for blame and revenge. It may take days, weeks or months, but the sooner you stop the blame and anger, the sooner you will be free to move on. Once you stop being angry at him, you will finally be free of his control.

Are you blaming yourself?

After blaming your ex, blaming yourself is the second most common way women deal with divorce. We, women, are very good at blaming ourselves for just about anything like it is our responsibility to hold the world on our shoulders. Whatever the reasons for divorce, you might be feeling the guilt for not being able to keep your marriage, for not being a better wife or mother. It is an overpowering sense of failure, of not doing what you were supposed to do.

Chapter 4

Many women feel depressed, feeling like their marriage failed because they were not worth loving or being married to. They feel that they could not keep their marriage because they were not good enough cooks, lovers, or housekeepers. Because they gained weight or lost weight, because they did not dress better or were unable to hold a conversation. Or any other nonsense. If only it was that easy to find the reasons for the end of a marriage.

You cannot accept total responsibility for the end of your marriage. You do not have that power or that responsibility. Neither does your husband. The blame game is ultimately pointless and does not produce any solution. Do not waste your energy or your time on it.

Chapter 5

It's Not A Secret

Getting a divorce for any reason is a time of turmoil, strong feelings, hurt, and insecurity. You want to scream with all bottled-up emotions and know that you need to talk to someone before your head explodes. But how can you possibly talk about the fact that your husband cheated on you with his secretary, or that he told you that you were boring or ugly or old or fat? Or that he spent all the family money gambling? Or that he hit you when he was drunk? Or even that you are so relieved to finally get out of that dreadful prison called marriage?

Misplaced shame

Shame is one of the main reasons so many women are reluctant to talk about their divorce. They feel that divorce is a sign of failure on their part, of the job they did not do well. They feel embarrassed that now that the divorce is final, all the dirt will come to light and everyone will learn about her misery. They often think that as a divorced woman they will be less worthy.

You do have to talk about all those bottled-up feelings but start first by talking to yourself. Whatever the reason for the divorce, you have to make up your mind about how much to say to whom.

Try not to play the role of a victim. Tell yourself that you are a strong, independent woman who already went through a lot and can deal with this latest bump in the road. Once you convince yourself of that, you can convey that feeling to others you talk to about your divorce. You will get a much different response than if you start by ranting about your ex, crying, or having angry bouts.

Refuse to feel sorry for yourself, and stop dwelling on the past and what should have been, because those past dreams are over.

Chapter 5

Now is the time for thinking about the future. Keep in mind that the purpose of this period of grieving, and talking about the divorce is part of it, has one purpose: to help you move on, take control of your life, and be happy again.

Start with a good, strong friend

Once you clear it all up with yourself, you will get a good idea of how to talk about your divorce. Start with someone you trust who loves you and knows you. Start with a good friend who was always there for you but is not too emotional and will be able to support you without feeling sorry for you or going around blabbing to other friends about your misfortune. You need a friend who will support you by making you feel stronger and in control and not encouraging your rants or feeling sorry for yourself.

If your friend is very close and already knew intimate details about your life and marriage, you can pour your heart out and bash your ex and his failings. Cry and rage and get it out of your system. But only if the friend is really close, can take it, and will put a stop to it if you keep going on and on.

All other friends and acquaintances should get just the basic information. Invite them for lunch in your favorite place and tell them that you and your husband decided to call it quits. Tell them that you are sad and hurt but that you are coping well and that you had things under control. Life goes on and you are optimistic about the future. That is the information you want to go out because it will. It will reach everyone in your circle and it is important that you control what they learn and will pass on. If you do not tell them the basic facts, they will come up with something.

Talking to the family

Hold off talking to your family until your emotions are a bit more under control. But, once you tell your friends about your divorce, the word will reach your parents and relatives.

If you are close to your parents, you probably told them about it before even talking to your friends. You can expect all sorts of reactions, including blaming you for the failure of your marriage. Your parents might consider him 'a good catch' and blame you for ruining it. Keep in mind that you did not share with them any information about his poor behavior, violence, drinking, or gambling. Don't be hurt by their reaction. Just tell them that divorce is best for everyone.

If you are lucky, your parents, siblings and relatives will be supportive and loving. They might offer to beat your ex up or to post his fake naked photos on the internet. Tell them that you are grateful for their support but that violence is not necessary. Tell them that you had things under control. Let them know that you prefer to keep the relationship civil for the sake of the kids and that it is not worth going to jail for your ex now that he is out of your life.

Talking to the kids

Talking to the kids is even more complicated, but it is urgent and crucial before they hear about their parents divorcing from their friends who overheard their parents talking about it. Kids can be cruel and might taunt your kids with lies and invented stories about the reasons for their parents' divorce, so it is very important that you prepare them for it. The last thing you want is for your kids to go into fights because some little brat told them some idiotic things about their parents.

Try to break the news about the divorce to the kids together with their father as mentioned earlier. That way, they will see that their parents are still together when it comes to them, even if they decided not to live together anymore. Whether you do it together or not, make sure that the kids know that their parents love them, and that the divorce is by no means their fault. In fact, it is nobody's fault, just life getting complicated and being together becoming more painful than being separated.

Don't expect the kids to accept it even if they do not react right away. Tell them that you are there for them to ask questions when they feel like it. Never bash their father. Never give them any sordid details. If they learn about their dad's new girlfriend, do not bash her either, little slut. Just tell them that you hope their dad will be happy with her. She might become their stepmom, so it's better to keep it civil.

Bell's story

Bell and her second husband decided to get a divorce. She knew that her husband was cheating on her with her best friend. She was hurt and betrayed, but she was not happy in the marriage and wanted it to end. She thought that the divorce would offer an opportunity to both of them to start from the beginning, while they still had time and were young enough to be happy again.

Bell had a son from her first marriage who loved his stepfather. They had a great relationship and he was his father in all sense of the word. Bell decided not to hurt that relationship by not telling her son about her husband's infidelity, but just to let him know that they decided to part amicably.

It was the right decision and pretty painless for everyone. Bell's son continued his relationship with his stepfather even after he remarried, never learning about him hurting his mom.

Be prepared for mixed reactions

Many of your friends and family members were and still are your husband's friends as well and they might find it necessary to take sides. Try to tell them that it is fine to stay friends with him, you will try to stay friends with him too even if you do not want to see his face ever again.

Always remember that you do not want to be seen as a victim. Do not let them feel sorry for you, that will only prevent you from moving on and seeing your life as getting better after the divorce, and not some catastrophe, even if it feels like it at times.

You will learn that many people you considered to be your friends are not really friends at all. They accepted you as part of a couple, a part of their social circle. Once you are 'a divorcee,' you do not fit in their world anymore. Many of them were your husband's friends and confidantes and knew that your marriage was over long before you. Some even knew about his philandering and covered for him. You do not need those kind of friends.

It is sad and you will feel hurt to see how many former friends are dropping out of your life and de-friending you from their Facebook and deleting your phone number. Good riddance. You are clearing the house anyway.

Tell your co-workers

You have to let your boss and your co-workers know about the divorce to control what goes around and to avoid gossiping and miscommunication. If you are emotionally distraught, take some time off but once back at work, behave professionally and avoid talking about it or becoming emotional.

Some old-fashioned companies have strict 'family policies,' encouraging and promoting family values. They might see your divorce as deviating from that policy, so you need to explain that the divorce is not your fault or your wish, but that you are coping with it and that it will not affect your performance.

You might find it amazing that in the 21st century, being a 'divorcee' has bad connotations. Not being a divorced man, it only applies to women. Ignore it if you can, it is primitive and barbaric. Being in a marriage is not a prerequisite for a happy and fulfilled life. Being divorced is not your job description or character trait.

Tell kids' teachers and coaches

You should tell your children's teachers, coaches, and daycare staff about the divorce. They might see the changes in the kids' behavior and should know the reasons for it. They should also know about your arrangements with your ex for picking up the kids after school or participating in school activities.

Talk to the counselor or therapist

Things do not always work out smoothly and you might feel alone, scared or insecure and in a need of professional advice. Ask your friends or your physician to recommend someone good.

Be open about your feelings when talking to professionals; they should know what is bothering you and what you need help with. Sometimes friends can help, but there are times when you need someone whose advice and help you can trust.

Often, just unburdening yourself by talking openly about your feelings will make you feel better. Your therapist will assure you that what you are going through is a part of the normal process of going through a traumatic experience. He or she will also be able to notice the signs of depression and treat them accordingly.

Join a support group

If you think it would help you to share your experience with other people in the same situation, join a divorce support group. Your physician or friends or priest might be able to recommend one.

It might make you feel better to hear other people tell their stories, burst into tears and air their family dirt in front of total strangers, or it might make you run for the door. It can be cathartic to unburden yourself to strangers you will never see again. At least they know exactly what you are going through.

Tell it all to your journal

Your journal can be your best friend during the worst time after the divorce. It is one place where you can tell everything, cursing and all. Try to describe in detail what happened, who said what and what you felt. Be totally honest with yourself and dig deep into what you are feeling and why. Nobody is going to read it; it is just for you. It will help you when you read it a few days later to see how your grief progresses slowly and surely toward closure.

Talk to your lawyer

If you are lucky to have a good lawyer who helped you go through the divorce with the least damage and some financial security, use that lawyer to help you with the aftermath as well. He or she is one person you can and should tell it all to, especially if your ex is giving you hard time or not sticking to the agreement.

It is much better to let the lawyer talk to your ex about disputes than to do it yourself. You do not need that aggravation and potential shouting match that will ensue. Avoid any opportunity to hit him with a hard object, it is illegal and the kids will not like it.

Whoever you are talking to about your divorce, always keep in mind that you are not a victim. You are a strong woman going through a difficult situation and you are coping the best you can, with the ultimate goal to heal and build a happy future.

Chapter 6

Developing A New Routine

There is this feeling of drifting without an anchor after the divorce. Remember walking through your home and wandering, "What now?" Nothing will ever be the same. Everything that you knew, planned, and dreamed of is now gone. You do not ever know who you are, where you belong and what is your purpose.

In the beginning, those thoughts will make you despondent and even depressed. But then small things will remind you that there are so many good things you can look forward to now. Like when you are making breakfast and you do not have to make eggs and bacon as your husband demanded every morning. You can make a smoothie or a bowl of cereal. Or have cake with your coffee for breakfast. And suddenly you will realize that not being married makes you free. Alone, but free.

Once you start seeing the opportunities being divorced offers, you will know that you are on the road to healing.

Do what you always wanted

Start by looking at all routines that made up your married life. Which of them did you hate? Having to wake up at six to make breakfast for your husband? Or having only dark-colored towels in the bathroom? Or the oh-so-traditional plaid bed sheets? Or visiting your mother-in-law every Sunday? Or having meat with every meal? Or having your hair in the elegant French twist?

Out with all that! You now do not report to anyone. Except maybe your kids, but they will be all for going a bit crazy.

Start with small things that are easy. They will give you the taste of freedom and encourage you to make some more meaningful and significant changes.

Chapter 6

Changing the house?

Kids need their routine after the divorce as too much change makes them insecure. Talk to them and explain how nice it would be to find a more modern or smaller or more interesting house or apartment. They usually only care to stay close to their friends, so if you make it sound fun, they will support you.

Often, the divorce agreement forces you to sell your bigger house and move to something smaller. Don't be sad about it. Everything about that big house only reminds you of your life with your husband. You built it for your life together. Even furniture and décor were a compromise between the two very different tastes.

Look at moving to the new place as an opportunity. Try to remember how you felt when you found your first apartment when you were younger—so much excitement and hope and anticipation. You can have it again. Go shopping for the furniture you like and paint walls the way you always wanted. Get your kids' paintings framed and ask your artistic friends to give you some of their art to put on your walls.

A new home usually means a new neighborhood and new neighbors. You will meet people who do not know your husband and who will not feel awkward talking to you and who will not be nosy about what happened to your marriage.

Time to meet some new friends

Now that you do not have to be home every evening to make dinner for your husband, you are free to join any club you want. Dancing salsa? Why not. Hiking? Mountain-climbing? Kickboxing? Mud wrestling? Why not all of them!

You might find that, after the divorce, going to the same clubs you did before is not the same anymore. Your tennis club is full of your 'friends' who were friends with your husband and who are now giving you a cold shoulder. Who needs them? You never liked the snobby atmosphere of that club anyway.

Changing the places you used to visit routinely will open your world to so many new opportunities. New clubs and new hobbies will make you meet new people. And if you choose hobbies and activities you are really passionate about, you will meet people who feel the same. That is such a great feeling, to have the same interest, the same passion, and the same way of spending your free time.

New hairdresser – new look!
Interestingly, getting a new look is not one of the first thoughts women have after a divorce. Probably because it is difficult enough to define their new role in this new life, and getting a new look feels like a bit much change. But think about it. When was the last time you had a haircut you wanted and not something you did to please your husband? Ages, right?

You might find that getting a short haircut or new color might make you feel free and brave and ready for anything. If your hairdresser is good, ask him or her what would be a really good look for you.

Kids might make fun of you if you come home with a punk look with green spikes, but tell them that they better get over it because that is their real mother hiding behind all that traditional costume.

Your favorite restaurant? Time to find a new one
So many couples get into a routine of going to the same places for dinner or lunch or when they want to celebrate something.

And if you go there now and if the waiter asks you if you wanted a table for two, you might want to scream at him.

Avoid all that, including the memories of lovely meals you had there with your husband. No use dwelling on that, it is what it is. Time to find some nice new spot just for you.

Look around your neighborhood for a place to have a cup of coffee or a plate of real homemade pasta or really good sushi. Maybe there is a nice wine bar that can become your new watering hole?

If you want to celebrate something, look at the reviews for the new restaurants, treat yourself and check them out. It might be outrageously expensive, but you only live once. Treat yourself and your best friend or the kids.

Get rid of the dreaded commute

Getting a new house or apartment is the perfect opportunity to look for a place close to your work. Walking or biking to work is a whole new way to experience your neighborhood or start your day. You are combining going to work with your morning exercise.

You will meet your neighbors, see which bakeries are open early by inhaling that heavenly smell of fresh bread, and find out what flowers grow well in your neighborhood. You will become aware of the change of seasons, watch the leaves turn red, and feel the sunrise on your face.

There are so many other advantages. You will not need a car, just rent one on the weekends if you want to go hiking. And not having a car means no car insurance and car maintenance. That is a lot of money in your pocket.

Get a dog!

If you always wanted a dog and your husband was allergic, pretending to be allergic, or hated pet hairs on the furniture, now you can fulfill your wish. Go to a shelter and pick up your new companion. Take the kids with you. They will love it.

Dogs, much more than cats, demand a lot of attention, but during this period when you are feeling a bit lonely and lost, having someone who will love you unconditionally is a great pleasure. Even the chores such as regular walks are to your advantage. They force you to walk out twice a day, breathe fresh air, meet other dog owners, and destress in a way that nothing else offers.

You can talk to a dog and pour out your soul and you will not be judged or given advice you do not want. Don't laugh. It works. All dog owners talk to their dogs although not all will admit it. So often all you need is someone to listen and dogs are really good at it.

Review your lifestyle

Did you have any strong political or environmental or religious feelings that you had to suppress after you got married because your husband did not share them? It happens so often. You might have stopped going to church because your husband was not religious or had a different religion. If religion was part of your upbringing, you might find it to be a great solace and comfort after the divorce.

If you had strong opinions about how we treat our environment, now is the time to express them. Start recycling, invest in solar energy, compost your organic refuse, and collaborate in the community garden. There are so many ways to be more environmentally conscious, and if you care, now you can find them.

Help where you can

Even while you are in the throes of feeling sorry for yourself, freshly after the divorce, you have to remind yourself that there are so many people who have it much worse. Helping others puts things into perspective and suddenly your divorce will not look like the end of the world. Your kids are not hungry, you have a job, a home, security, and good health.

There might be a soup kitchen in your neighborhood, a community garden that needs help, or the local school needs parents to help with evening activities or school outings. Maybe your old neighbor needs help with getting groceries. Look around. Get out of your personal bubble and see the world around you. There is so much you can contribute.

Are you happy with your job?

Shortly after the divorce is not a good time to start looking for another job, but you might want to start thinking about whether your job is satisfying you. You might feel like you have more to offer than the routine, boring admin job. Think about what you would really like to do and start planning how to get it. Going back to school is one good way. Look for online courses to start with. Later, you might want to go to some real classes and meet other students.

Mell's story

The first thing Mell did after her divorce was to start planning to go back to school. She even managed to convince her husband during the divorce proceeding to fund it. To her surprise, he agreed. She found a number of online courses she could do at night after the kids were asleep.

Because she was studying for her degree in environmental sciences, she had to take some practical courses in the field. She dreaded having to go with other students the age of her children, but she found that she truly enjoyed it. They went hiking through forests, collecting samples of trees or watching birds trying to identify them. Young people's enthusiasm was contagious and made courses much more pleasant for Mell. She managed to get her degree in a record time and was able to secure a job in the field soon after.

Changes mean growth

Once you start getting rid of old routines and developing new ones, you will realize that you are thriving. You will find yourself too busy to dwell on your failed marriage. Starting so many new, interesting things will show you that your life is not over but just beginning. You will feel like a caterpillar who is ready to turn into a butterfly.

While changes can be painful and scary, if you are the one choosing the kind of changes you are making, you are in control. You can always stop doing what you find that you are not enjoying and do something else.

Much of what is happening to you after the divorce can be seen as 'mind over matter,' a good way of coping with an unpleasant situation. If you are determined to move on and be happy with your new life, you will be. The mind is a powerful thing.

Even small changes you make in your routines after the divorce are the changes you choose, and they build your self-confidence and self-determination. They will show you just how strong, resilient, and powerful you are. You can do it. There is a whole new life ahead of you.

Chapter 7

THE KEY TO LETTING GO - WHAT IF I STILL CAN'T LET GO?

After your divorce, you heard so many well-meaning people telling you: just let it go. Like you would not if you could. But you cannot. You feel like your self-confidence has taken quite a beating, and it was not strong at the best of times.

You feel like your divorce is just one more sign of how miserable your life is. You feel betrayed, lonely, and depressed, and cannot even think about what next life will throw at you. Move on to what, exactly? Empty house, empty bank account, zero employment opportunity after years of being a housewife.

So often, divorce comes in the throes of a midlife crisis. It is the period of life when one or both partners contemplate their future and are not happy with what they have, so divorce is a solution they come up with. Midlife crisis is hard enough to deal with on so many levels, but combined with divorce, it can create a seriously messy situation.

There are many reasons some women find it hard or impossible to move on and contemplate happy and fulfilling life after divorce:

- The reason for a divorce keeps them feeling furious;
- Deep trauma caused by the unexpected betrayal of the one person they truly trusted and counted on;
- Seeing divorce as one more sign of being a victim of life's unfairness;
- Suffering from low self-esteem;
- Going through a difficult mid-life crisis;
- A sense of loneliness;
- Pre-existing mental health issues such as anxiety or depression;
- Alcoholism or other substance abuse.

Chapter 7

Even one of these issues can make moving on difficult if not impossible. If more than one combines, life looks bleak and the future very difficult to contemplate.

The first thing to do on the way to recovery is to remember that you are not alone in this mess. Many women have been where you are today and managed to pull themselves out. Here are some tried and trusted tips and tricks to help you along the way:

1. Work on acceptance

When you decided to get married, you did not think that you would get divorced. Nobody does, except people insisting on a prenuptial agreement. Rationally, you know that about half the number of marriages end in divorce, but you believed it is not going to happen to you. You are each other's soul mate, meant for each other. So when the end comes, it hits you like a ton of bricks.

Women naturally think about all the things they should have done better, something that would have prevented their marriage from ending. How could this even be possible? You are confused and lost and find it very hard to accept that it happened to you.

But it did. It is the hard fact: your marriage is over and you have to find a way to accept it and deal with it. All those 'If only…" and "How could he just destroy what we had?" or "But we love each other so much," are only holding you back and not helping. You have to leave the past in the past.

Try telling yourself:

- "OK, I hate it, but it happened and there is nothing I can do to change it."

67

- "All my lovely plans for the life I was to have are now dead, but I can make new plans. My life is not over."

Don't expect to just accept your divorce and the new reality easily and quickly. There are intense emotions involved, and many of your dreams and plans now have to be completely revised. It takes time. Give yourself a break.

Treat yourself nicely and kindly. You are a good person in a messy situation that you did not plan on and do not deserve. It will get easier with time.

2. All your feelings are normal

As you slowly come to terms with your divorce, you will be flooded with intense emotions that might linger for some time:

- Betrayal;
- Pain;
- Sadness;
- Fear;
- Doubt;
- Uncertainty;
- Disgust;
- Anger;
- Hostility;
- Grief;
- Regret;
- Loss;
- Relief;
- Peace;
- Loneliness and many others.

All those feelings are normal and it is also normal that you feel more than one, some really conflicting. You are furious with your ex for leaving you for his secretary, but you also love and miss him.

If you wanted out of your marriage because it was abusive and unhappy, you might feel relief, but also regret and a sense of failure.

Whatever you are feeling, accept it; all those feelings are normal, although exhausting.

There are some practices that help deal with intense and often confusing emotions:

- Learn to practice mindfulness—being in the moment. It means focusing on all the sensations coming to you through your senses at a particular moment: smells, sounds, textures, views, and tastes. Not what is churning through your mind. There are easy videos to get you going, the rest is practice.
- Make meditation part of your routine. It is easy to learn the basics by watching a video or you can join a nearby club. It is really helpful when dealing with intense emotions. And with anything else actually;
- If you catch yourself endlessly chewing on what happened and what you should and could have done, just stop it and distract yourself by doing something else, such as watching a movie, going for a walk, calling a good friend;
- If you have a hard time controlling your emotions, think of them as something created by your mind. And if the mind created them, your mind can control them. We will talk more about controlling emotions in the chapter about tools you need to deal with the mess you find yourself in.

3. Develop a co-parenting plan

If you have children, it is one of your main concerns: how are they dealing with divorce and how is a divorce going to impact their future? You understand from what you heard from friends and what you read that children deal with divorce much better if both parents agree on working together on taking care of them.

There is a lot of research on this topic because of its importance. Scientists found that, to achieve emotional, physical, and behavioral health, children should spend at least 35 percent of their time with each of their parents.

Working together to help children go through a divorce without permanent scars is in everyone's interest. If it works well, parents and children have a better chance of having a healthy relationship after divorce.

To avoid any issues and problems, parents need to develop a plan for when and for how long each parent spends with their children. It should cover weekends, vacations, holidays, visits to grandparents, and anything else. It is not a competition; it is what both parents and children need. Once the plan is developed, both parents should honor it and be flexible when some change is inevitable without looking for a secret motivation.

Children should also have a say in how much time they want to spend with each parent. If for some reason they refuse to visit their father, or prefer to live with their father when they are supposed to live with their mother, parents should consult a family counselor or a therapist to get to the real reason for this. Kids might not be able or not be willing to verbalize it, or even might not be aware of the real reason.

Chapter 7

Think of your kids' needs. If they are happy, you will be happy. Put your issues with your ex to the side. If he loves his kids and they love him, you should be happy about it.

A co-parenting plan includes other issues besides scheduled visits:

- Both parents should follow the same rules for bedtime, homework time, and time spent with electronics;
- The same goes for what happens if the kids break the rules. Playing the 'good guy' when kids misbehave is not in their interest;
- Kids might try to avoid doing their chores and other responsibilities when visiting the other parent. Don't let them get away with it, little brats;
- There should be strict rules on staying in contact and reporting any issues;
- Parents should agree on what to tell their kids about the divorce. Hearing two different stories from different parents will make them lose confidence in their parents and think that there are hidden things they are not told about. Don't forget that most kids believe that divorce is somehow their fault.

Working together on parenting your children even when you do not live together anymore gives children a message that they are still loved by both parents and that they will continue to take care of them.

4. Keep your temper under control when communicating with your ex

Regardless of how much you loathe your ex and how you hate having anything to do with him after divorce, screaming at him every time you have to communicate will solve nothing. Be calm and controlled and you will be able to deal with issues much better.

It does not mean that you have to stop loathing him. It is your given right. Just keep it to yourself when you have to deal with any important details, in person or on the phone.

A few rules that help:

- Make sure that there are set rules and boundaries for who calls when, for what or how. What should be done by email, WhatsApp, text, or in person. What are the reasons that merit any type of communication? Be assertive and clear about it to avoid unnecessary confrontations.
- Deal with facts and necessary responsibilities when communicating, like kids' care, finances, and such.
- Control the urge to insult him, be snarky, or hurtful. Do not allow it if he tries. Any attempt should be the reason to terminate the conversation.
- Listen to what he has to say, it is probably something important. Insist that he hears you as well. Be assertive, even if you were never before while you were married. You might as well start learning how to do it.

5. Have some fun with your children

You and your children are starting a new chapter in your life. You might have lost some habits, customs and routines you had before, so you should start developing the new ones. The more fun you have together, the easier it will be for all of you to go through this painful transition phase.

You need to find enough time, and energy, to spend quality time with your children, even if it is just watching a movie on TV together and chatting about the day they had. It is not fair to them to allow your feelings, anxiety, and depression to deprive them of your love and care.

It does not have to be fun and games all the time. Making pancakes for breakfast together can be enough.

Try to establish new, pleasant routines:

- Once a week, go to the park, see a movie, go to the zoo or volunteer at the animal shelter;
- New rituals should be something they will look forward to, such as playing a board game once a week or going to their favorite restaurant or arcade;
- If possible, have dinner together every day and let the kids talk freely about the day they had. It will help you learn if something is bothering them. Sometimes, the time in the car while you are driving them serves the same purpose.

Encourage kids to ask any questions they have about the divorce, but do not force it. If they ask, be honest without going into any details and give them the information you think is appropriate for their age. Always answer calmly and do not let them provoke you if they try to take their father's side.

Never talk badly about their father and do not allow them to do so.

What they learn about divorce, marriages, and relationships from you will be their guide for their future relationships.

6. Spend time with those who love you

You will most likely prefer to be alone during the first period after you learned about your divorce, while your emotions are all over the place and you feel lost and confused. But never forget that you are not alone and that there are people who love you and who are there for you.

Those who love you, your support system, are your team, your cheering squad, people who will listen to you and understand you. With them, you can be you. It is very liberating and healing to understand that. Let them help.

Sometimes, the best help friends and family can offer is to listen and let you rant. Those who went through the same experience will have more empathy and understanding. Your support team can also be there for you for more practical issues such as babysitting, financial advice, help with money if needed, and even letting you stay with them.

Be careful who you include in your support team. You do not need anyone who is judgmental, even if it is a close family. You need support, not a judge and jury.

7. It is a good time for some new friends

Besides dividing your furniture and other belongings, you and your ex probably had to split your friends as well. You probably found that some friends you thought were yours are actually your husband's. Never mind. You are starting so many new things in your life, you might as well add some new friends.

There are some good ways to meet new potential friends:

- Join a volunteer group in your neighborhood;
- Invite a co-worker you like to coffee, lunch, or a morning walk;
- Join a class in crafts, music, art, cooking, or sports.
- Join a local divorce support group.

8. Get to know yourself again

It is fairly common to lose a sense of self during marriage. As the marriage ends, you might start wondering who on earth you are now.

It is inevitable to change to an extent during the marriage, to adapt to living with another person. You might have stopped doing things you liked because they interfered with your married life. Sometimes, you changed quite a lot to please your husband.

Now that the marriage is over you are free to reexamine yourself and see who you have become, do you like that new self or do you want to shake it up a bit. Try to remember things you used to like and do regularly. You are totally free to be yourself, so examine what it means.

Would you like to:

- spend more time outdoors and not in a gym;
- be vegetarian;
- live in a modern small apartment instead of a big mansion;
- go to sleep early or spend the night working and then sleep late;
- dig out your easel and paints and get to work;
- get rid of your fashionable clothes and live in yoga pants;
- get a dog or a cat.

Really, the sky is the limit. Just run it by your kids first.

9. Start new routines

So many things changed with your divorce. Most of your routines do not exist anymore. No wonder you feel lost and without an anchor. Without familiar routines, you tend to ruminate the past and run on an endless loop of memories of things you used to do and enjoy doing with your ex. To avoid all that and the inevitable sense of loneliness, you need to keep busy and start new routines.

- Create small new rituals that give you pleasure. Take a break for tea and get a nice set of tea cups. Maybe some new loose-leaf tea you always liked. Or start doing yoga on your porch every morning;
- Learn about creating a self-care routine. Nobody tells married women about the self-care routine—a set of daily activities to support your physical, emotional, and spiritual needs. We will talk more about that in the chapter on tools for going through a divorce.
- Transform your ex's 'man cave' into your sanctuary. Get fluffy curtains, candles and colorful cushions. Or make it totally Zen. Whatever works for you. If you are moving to a new place, find a spot that will serve as your sanctuary, even if it is your bathroom.
- Start a new bedtime routine. You are probably not sleeping well, as your mind is churning about the past and the future. Help yourself sleep better by creating a soothing and relaxing sleeping environment. Get the bed linen you enjoy, get some aroma therapy, have a hot bath, or put on some relaxing music. To avoid running like mad in the morning,

prepare for the morning in advance by putting your coffee machine and bread machine on a timer. Take out the clothes you need for tomorrow. Prepare kids' lunches in advance.

+ Find time for some kind of physical activity you enjoy. It can be just walking the dog, hiking, swimming, or running up the stairs.

10. Resist the blaming game

Whatever the reason for the end of your marriage, it is tempting to find someone to blame: yourself or your ex. But if you are honest with yourself, there are always two parties in this dance. Even if your ex was an abusive monster, you stayed with him and allowed him to continue the abuse.

Whatever the case, you played at least some part in it. Now, when the emotions are high, you are not ready to see things from his point of view. But eventually, you will. You will see that people, including you, change with time and with circumstances. And often, with time, you realize that you did not really know the person you married. Love tends to make us blind.

You can rationally analyze your marriage and see the reasons why it failed: lack of communication, incompatibility, mental health issues, alcoholism or whatever. But assigning blame does not help any of that. And it will keep you from moving on. What happened is in the past. All you can do is learn from it and make sure you do not make the same mistake in the future.

11. Wait a bit before starting a new relationship

You might be tempted to throw yourself into a steaming romance or just a quick hookup after the divorce, but it can backfire and is ultimately unsatisfying for a range of reasons.

You might end up:

- Talking endlessly about your ex to your new partner;
- comparing him to your ex;
- treating the new relationship as temporary and not giving it a chance to be anything more even if it deserves it;
- you might be falling into the same trap and ignoring your physical and mental needs to satisfy your new partner.

Even if you feel lonely, and never lived alone, give it a try after the divorce; it is therapeutic. You cannot try to find a new partner before you have the time to find yourself first.

12. Work with a professional

Try to recognize the signs that you are not coping well and that you need help dealing with all issues your divorce forced you to face. A therapist is a professional you can talk to openly and honestly and who can help you find the best way to cope with any issues such as:

- long-lasting and pervasive grief;
- self-doubt;
- feelings of guilt and failure;
- rage, anger, and irritability;
- depression.

Getting professional help will help you get out of the post-divorce grief faster and move on, ready for the new future. It will also help you deal with children and help them cope, perform better at work, and establish a new healthy routine.

Most importantly, a professional will be able to tell you that you are going through the normal phases of such a huge event in your life, how best to cope with them and how to recognize when what you are feeling is not normal and requires more help. If anxiety and depression are not treated in time, they can become chronic mental issues and interrupt your normal life for a long time.

If all the suggested keys to letting go look to you like lessons you need to learn before you can move to the new life, they probably are. Each step and each thing you do for yourself will make you more ready to move on and embrace happiness again.

Chapter 8

Strengthening Your Defenses

Not everyone is born strong, resilient, and self-confident. Most of us learn those basic life skills along the way. But the time we learn fastest is when we are in crisis when those skills make the difference between coping successfully and falling into deep depression and despondency.

Fortunately, life skills are skills like any others and can be learned. Look at them as your armor against the hard reality, pain, and uncertain future. You can boost your armor and your defenses and those skills will greatly help you get out of this stressful phase of your life stronger, better for the experience and ready for a better and happier future. These skills will serve you forever and will help you deal with whatever life throws at you in the future.

Develop a self-care routine

American writer, feminist, librarian, and civil rights activist, Audre Lorde said that "Caring for myself is not self-indulgence, it is self-preservation." Considering how vital this skill is for anyone dealing with the vagaries of modern living, it is shocking how few women actually know how to take care of themselves. Taking care of children, husband, home, career, and parents, that is all normal and accepted. But when it comes to self-care, most women do not have time or think that they are fine without it.

Well, they are not. And it shows painfully and clearly when they hit an obstacle such as divorce.

What is self-care?

The Oxford Dictionary defines self-care as "the practice of taking an active role in protecting one's well-being and happiness, in particular during periods of stress."

Chapter 8

Self-care consists of habits that you have to develop and then practice every day. They are meant to support and nurture all aspects of your health and well-being. Your self-care routine will allow you to feel calmer and more balanced each day, even in the middle of a stressful period such as divorce.

The habits included in your self-care routine are nothing special or new. They are things you already enjoy doing, that give you pleasure and make you feel de-stressed. What makes them a part of your self-care is the fact that you have to make them into habits and practice them every day. It means that you need to take a part of your day and make it purely yours, your special time when you care for all your needs.

Many of the activities take only 15 minutes or so, so they will not become just another chore in your already full list. But it is vital that you find the time for yourself and do those activities every day.

Self-care activities

You are a complex human being. Your well-being depends on several aspects: physical, mental, emotional, social, and spiritual. You need to combine activities that support all your needs.

Choose the activities that suit you best, and that give you the benefits you need most. Many activities cover more than one need.

Physical activities boost the production of the hormone endorphin, a 'feel-good hormone.' Get on your bike, hit the trails, swim, dance, go rollerblading or skating, jump on a trampoline, play tennis or basketball, anything that will get your blood flowing. Get enough sleep, drink a lot of water, and eat balanced meals.

Spiritual needs are best boosted through mindful meditation. This ancient practice will change the way your body and mind work together. It will help you relax and reduce stress, anxiety, and depression. Join a group, look for help from an expert or learn the basics from one of many videos. Use positive affirmations to get more spiritual help. Remind yourself of all things you should be grateful for.

Don't neglect your **social needs**. We, humans, are social creatures and belonging to a tribe or group is part of our DNA, even if we are total introverts. Spend time with your favorite people, cook, play, dance, or laugh with them. Choose people that make you feel good—positive, supportive friends only. Do something nice for someone else; volunteer, or help someone in need.

There are so many ways to fulfill your **emotional needs**. Spend time with your pets. Talk to them. Take a dog for a walk, play with your or your neighbor's cat, and watch the fish swimming and hamster running endlessly. Laugh out loud. Get a movie, a funny book, or talk to a funny friend. Laughter increases oxygen in your blood, stimulates your heart, lungs and muscles, increases the production of endorphins, and boosts the immune system. Do something nice for yourself—get your hair done, go to a concert, buy a new book.

When you are designing your self-care routine, pick an activity from each category and try to see if they work. Spend just 15 minutes a day doing something for yourself, for each of your needs.

You can choose which activity to include in the routine, or change them if they do not work or you are not enjoying them. You decide, it is your life and your well-being. You will be surprised how much better you will feel if you persist and do this every day.

Let's see how it looks in practice. Let's say you are a morning person. Get up half hour before you would normally. Go for a run, walk, or swim. Go with a friend or take a dog. When you come back home, take a bath with some nicely smelling bath salt. Put some candles around the bathtub. Put some soothing music on. You can do your meditation exercise in the tub, or do it after. Focus on your breathing, clear your mind or all busy thoughts and plans for the day. Try to listen to the music only, smell the candles, feel the warm water on your skin. You will feel your breathing slowing and your mind clearing.

All that does not have to take more than half hour. You can do it in the evening if you prefer. You can pick an activity you like most. Eventually, you will find a set of activities that work for you and will enjoy doing them every day. Treasure that special time, it will keep you sane. Tell kids to leave you alone and respect your solitude.

Controlling emotions

We all experience a range of emotions every day of our lives. We often feel like slaves to our emotions, exhausted from their power to make us exhilarated, furious, afraid, expectant, or anything in-between.

Situations such as divorce are packed with emotions, and being able to control them would really feel good right now. You do not want to go all bothered every time you see your ex, or start screaming at him in front of the kids or bursting to tears at the drop of the hat. It is so tiring and ultimately makes you feel ashamed, embarrassed, weak, and out of control.

The key to controlling emotions is to accept that we all have them, that both good and bad emotions are normal and that it is in our power to control how we express them.

While scientists do not agree about the source of emotions, the prevalent theory is that our emotions actually come from our minds. Our emotions are a reaction to how our mind evaluates the situation we find ourselves in. Sounds confusing? Try to think of situations in which different people had completely different reactions: indifferent, afraid, excited. Remember going to a cave? Or riding a kayak on white waters?

When we find ourselves in a certain situation, such as meeting our ex, our mind evaluates it as threatening, informative, useful, helpful, mean, or anything else. And based on that evaluation, it causes us to feel a certain way: angry, anxious, expectant, or hopeful. You can control that by thinking about that meeting in advance and deciding how you are going to respond. Once prepared, and ready for anything he might say to provoke you, you will be able to have the response that benefits you: calm, informative, helpful, and assertive.

It is not easy and it takes practice, but controlling how you react to any situation is a skill you will be able to use in any stressful situation in life. Practice it; it gets easier with time. It is important not to suppress emotions. You are who you are; you have the right to feel the way you feel. Just suppress your outside reaction to your emotions. Be in control and in charge.

Boosting resilience

Resilience is defined as the ability to adapt and bounce back from hardships. We all go through challenges. Nobody is spared difficult situations, and nobody can protect us from them. What we need is to build up our defenses to deal with them, the inner strength we can tap into when faced with difficulties.

There are very few situations that challenge our resilience as divorce. Some people just collapse. Others suffer through pain, betrayal, insecurity, and loss of self to emerge on the other side stronger than ever.

There are different forms of resilience:

- Bouncing back quickly;
- Holding your head up through it all;
- Trying your best;
- Being strong on the inside;
- Being able to shrug it off;
- Being able to stand on your own.

Love conquers all

Most people build their innate resilience as children in their families. Love from your parents, siblings, friends, grandparents, teachers, or your dog is the first and the biggest shield you have against any future adversity.

You know that they love you unconditionally, even with your pimples, bad behavior and all, and it gives you a solid foundation from which you can face the world. They will always be there for you. They show you that you are worthy of love, a special person, strong and powerful.

High expectations

People who love you expect a lot from you. Not to be the prettiest, most successful or to have the most money. They expect, and you do too, to be a good human being, to always do your best, to respect others and to expect respect in return, to always be accountable for your actions, and to never do anything to hurt others. These expectations make you who you are—the best you can be.

You can be resilient and vulnerable at the same time

Being resilient means enjoying your life to the fullest. It means often taking risks, trying new things, experiencing all sorts of feelings and becoming richer for the experience. You expect to get hurt, but every challenge makes you bounce back even stronger.

Becoming more resilient

There are things you can do to boost your resilience:

- **Stay connected.** Having a strong support system means you have a circle of people you can count on if the need arises. They can be there for you to listen, support you, offer guidance or a hot meal. Just knowing that they are there is part of your resilience, your feeling of assurance that you will be able to cope.
- **Find meaning in every day.** Try to find a purpose for every day, something that will give you a sense of accomplishment. Make sure your goals are achievable, clear, and measurable.
- **Learn from every experience.** Every time you go through a stressful or difficult situation, think about what you can learn from it. How did you cope with it? Could you do better in the future? What would be the best strategy to use? Being prepared makes you less stressed.

- **Stay hopeful.** Accept that you cannot change the past, but you can prepare for the future being hopeful and positive. Accepting changes will make you more ready for them and more resilient.
- **Take care of your body and mind.** Staying healthy will make you better prepared to deal with difficulties. Try to be physically active, eat well, get enough sleep, and use ways to distress such as yoga and meditation.
- **Act proactively.** Don't wait for problems to show their ugly heads. Think about what has to be done to prevent them and do it. If you have looked for the signs of problems in your marriage, you would have dealt with them or better prepared for the collapse of the marriage.

Building self-confidence

Your self-confidence is the way you see yourself, how you look, feel and act, and who you are. Being confident means feeling good about who you are and being comfortable with yourself. This sense of self changes with time and experiences. During the marriage, especially if it was long, the idea you have of who you are might have changed.

This feeling of self is your own estimate and it is not necessarily accurate and it is not always how others see you. But, what you think about yourself is much more important than what others think about you, whether it is good or bad.

After the divorce, you might have to re-learn who you are, or who you have become. You need to evaluate your best qualities, and what you like and dislike about yourself at that particular time.

You might need help with that because when you are feeling low, your opinion of yourself might not be accurate. Talk to those who know you and love you. Ask them to make a list of your qualities. It is pretty likely that you will find more qualities than if you have made that list yourself. And it will make you think that you are not as bad as you feel right then or the way your ex makes you feel.

There are three parts to self-confidence:

+ *Competence* – what you believe about your skills and how you deal with any given situation;
+ *Resilience* – how adaptable you are to any changes and challenges;
+ *Optimism* – how hopeful you are that everything will get better.

Our confidence can get a beating for different reasons. Your ex might call you stupid, but if you know that you are smart, his insult will not touch you. But if you doubt your intelligence, this will hurt you very much and your confidence will nosedive. As long as you know your weaknesses, you can build your defenses and resistance to being hurt.

There are exercises you can do to boost your self-confidence.

Set yourself positive goals

This activity will help you see that you are able to achieve the goals you set for yourself.

These goals have to be realistic so you are actually able to do them. ("I will complete that puzzle tonight.")

Try to make your goals measurable, so you can see the result, and sufficiently important.

Set goals that are challenging and require effort. Achieving them will make you feel good about yourself.

Overcome negative beliefs

Negative experiences make you start doubting yourself and who you are. If your ex calls you names, you might start believing him. Write down all your negative beliefs ("I am lazy," or "I am useless").

Give your list to someone you trust and who knows you (your parents, best friend). Ask them to write a comment about each of your negative beliefs. Ask them to help you change these negative beliefs and make them more realistic and constructive. You will see that you are not as bad as you thought.

Appreciate yourself

Write down a list of what you believe are your good qualities. If you cannot think of any because the divorce made you doubt you have any, try answering these questions:

- What do I like about myself? (Combine different qualities such as character, looks, and achievements.)
- Which three or four words would describe me best?
- What are my skills and talents?
- If I met a person who is just like me, what would I like about that person?

Show the answers to these questions to your parents, sister, or a best friend, and ask them what they think are your best qualities.

It is very likely that your family's list is much longer than yours. It will tell you a lot about how others see you. Think about it and try to believe what your loved ones tell you.

Motivation for the day

We spoke before about the motivation jar or box. Fill it up with positive motivations and pick one up from the jar every morning, to guide you along the way.

The board of achievements

During your marriage, you might have forgotten about your previous achievements and the things you have achieved during your marriage probably did not get enough notice. Well, get them all out. Find a board of some kind and stick on it all proofs of your achievements: diplomas, certificates, ribbons, photos of your victories or your best pie, a scarf you knitted or a photo of a puppy you saved from the shelter.

Keep the board somewhere where you can see it and remind yourself of your achievements. Encourage kids to add to it. Let it remind you of who you are and what you are capable of. Nobody can take it from you.

Chapter 9

IF YOU ARE THE ONE TO INITIATE DIVORCE

There are so many reasons marriages end in divorce: you discovered that you did not know the person you married at all, personality clashes, falling out of love, infidelity, inequality in the relationship, money, unrealistic expectations, a lack of commitment and so many other reasons.

If you are the one who initiated the divorce, you would expect that it would be a relief, a sense of freedom and expectations of better things to come. Instead, you feel guilt and shame, even if a divorce is the best option for everyone involved.

Unless your ex was abusive, it is normal to feel guilty if your spouse or partner does not feel the same as you. It is the person that you once loved and hoped to live with 'until death do you part.' You do not like to see him hurt. There are a few things to help you cope with this painful outcome of your decision

Be compassionate

Even if you and your ex discussed the possibility of divorce as your marriage deteriorated, it might come as a shock to him when you actually go ahead and initiate the divorce proceedings. You can expect resistance even if you know that divorce is the best solution for both of you.

You can expect emotional outbursts, anger, denial, and refusal to agree to the divorce. He is likely feeling hurt, or his pride is hurt that he was not the one to start it. He might be thinking of the divorce as a mistake and that you should have tried to repair the relationship. Or he might be angry at you believing you to be unfaithful and refusing to believe that it is not the truth.

Try to understand his feelings and do not respond to his emotional outbursts, but do not allow him to be abusive or violent. Try to explain without emotions that your decision is something that you should discuss and that would allow both of you to move on and have a chance to have a better relationship with someone else in the future. Explain that you thought about your decision long and hard and that you took everything into consideration before deciding that divorce is the best option.

Keep the communication flowing

Keeping the lines of communication open during the divorce proceedings is crucial and it usually helps heal the wounds faster. Allow your spouse to express his concerns. Accept his feelings of hurt and pain and even surprise if he did not realize that you were serious about the divorce when you discussed it before.

Keep the dialogue regardless of how painful it is to you as long as your spouse is not abusive and refuses to accept the reality of the end of the marriage. Try to discuss practical things involved in the breakup of the marriage in a rational way, such as sharing of property or the care of the kids. The more helpful and patient you are, the faster this first stage of grief will be over.

Discuss your partner's objections to a divorce

Allow your partner to tell you exactly why he is so opposed to divorce. Answer each of his objections rationally and without emotions. Explain that divorce is better for the kids than a bad marriage that will affect how they form relationships in their lives. Try to discuss each of his objections as long as he remains rational and non-abusive. Hopefully, your answers to his objections will eventually sink in and convince him that the divorce is the right decision for him as well, once he stops feeling hurt.

Give your partner time

The end of the marriage is painful and you feel the pain even if you are the one who initiated its end. Just imagine how your partner feels. Give both yourself and him time to adjust to this new reality and accept that it is time to move on. He might need time to process his feelings and you should be patient and give him space to grieve.

Try not to be judgmental. You are getting what you wanted, he did not. You had time to adjust to the idea while you were trying to make the decision, but your partner did not. He might be dealing with the shock and feel betrayed, hurt and lonely. Grief takes time to process. Eventually, he will come to terms with it. If not, there are counselors you can ask for help.

Look for help when needed

If your partner is taking too long to accept your decision or flatly refuses to participate in the divorce proceedings, look for a counselor in your area. It might be late for marriage counseling, but talking to a professional who can help your partner come to terms with the divorce in a rational and unemotional way might be useful. Men often feel wounded pride and they feel differently when a neutral professional is involved.

Once it is over

The pain and hurt your ex feels might continue after the divorce becomes final. If there are children, do your best to convince him to stay friendly for their sake and share parenting duties. If you are separating property, let him have things that are dear to him. It is funny how much friendlier men can become if you let him have his giant TV.

Chapter 9

Accept that your ex will be hurt and will take longer to adjust to the new reality than you, but do not allow him to guilt you for the divorce. You did not make that decision lightly and your marriage would not have ended if it worked for both of you. He might not have been ready for it, but you were and you have the right to move on without feeling guilty.

If he wants to get together to discuss some practical issues, feel free to accept a meeting for lunch, but only if you are comfortable with it. If he just wants to meet 'for old time's sake' and you do not, feel free to refuse.

If you are worried about how your ex is coping with the divorce, talk to a common friend or his relative that you are close to. Ask them to help because he might be reluctant to do so. Talking to his parents might not be a good idea; they might blame you for the whole mess.

Keep in mind that your ex is an adult and that he is capable of taking care of himself, even if you were the one to take care of all his needs for years. It is not your job. It never was, but now you really do not have to feel sorry for him going around in a dirty shirt. He better learn to take care of himself, hire someone or, most likely, he will get into a new relationship and repeat the same pattern that caused your marriage to end.

Chapter 10

Learning to be Alone

There are women who simply cannot imagine living alone. You might be one of them. If you left your parents' home to live in a dorm in a college with someone and then got married, you have in effect never lived alone. And you dread it. So you see divorce as the time that will force you to be totally alone. What a dread. You feel like the floor is shifting under your feet.

Other women need a man to complete them. They cannot imagine living alone. They feel inadequate and without a purpose. You might be one of those.

Our society is designed for couples, like it or not, so being alone and enjoying it is not normal. But it can be wonderful if you decide to make it so. After the pain of accepting that your marriage is over and that you now have to come up with a whole new life, you find yourself alone, thinking of what to do with yourself. The trick is to stop thinking of being alone as a bad thing. Because it has so many good sides. All you have to do is go ahead and start enjoying them. Here are **some ideas:**

You are not responsible for him anymore

Most women are trained to 'take care of their husband.' It means you made sure his laundry is done, he does not forget the kids or his mother's birthdays, or what to wear for the office party. You made his meals, cleaned his house, and raised his kids. You practically ran his life.

Instead of feeling purposeless now that you do not have to do any of that for him, try to enjoy the fact that you now do not have to be responsible for him. Who cares whether he has clean clothes or does not know how to clean his new apartment? Feeling sorry for him? You silly girl. That was never your job, you just accepted it. He is just going to find a girlfriend to do all those chores. Don't be jealous, she will find out soon enough what she is in for.

The smell of freedom

Right after the divorce, you will feel totally alone, and the house will feel empty. You will be scared of not being able to deal with whatever the future is bringing. But just remember that being alone also means that you are free to do whatever you want.

How many times have you had to compromise when planning to do anything while married, often ending up not doing or getting what you wanted? Now you can do whatever you want. Even that freedom will feel scary in the beginning. But it will pass, once you start practicing it. Want to go to Bali? Book that trip. Want to cut your hair (which your husband claimed was your best feature)? Cut it off!

Are you actually alone?

Not being married does not mean you are alone in life. You have kids, parents, relatives, friends, officemates, so many people in your life who care for you. Actually, now that you are free to think of them, you realize that you neglected them because they did not fit in your married life, you were too busy being married or your husband did not like them. Now you can get to really enjoy them. Go visit them, invite them to your house or a restaurant. You will find out that not only you are not alone, but you are not lonely at all.

Nobody is responsible for your happiness

If you count on others, even the man you loved, to make you happy, you are on the path of disappointment. You have to be your own source of happiness. You do not need anyone to fulfill you. How you see yourself is in you. It does not mean that other people in your life do not make you happy, they do, but they are not in your life to do that.

If you totally depended on your ex to make you happy, you will be doubly miserable after divorce because you will feel like your only source of happiness is gone. So, get to know yourself again and find that inner source of happiness that was always there. Maybe that is what being alone is for.

Do not allow yourself time to think too much about being alone

If you expect to be lonely after divorce, you will stay home alone and feel sorry for yourself. But if you decide to use your alone time to have some fun, you can have as much of it as you want.

Remember all those hobbies you had before you got married? You used to like to paint, or write, or knit, or play with clay or ride horses. Guess what? You can and should do all that. Not only will you enjoy yourself, but you will also remind yourself how good you are at so many things—a serious booster to your self-esteem.

Try something new

Trying new things has several purposes. One is to challenge yourself and conquer that fear of being inadequate, stupid, lazy, slow, or whatever. Now that you are alone, you do not have to prove anything to anyone.

Try new things even if you are not good at them. Who cares? After you try enough of them, you will surely find something you are good at and are enjoying so much that it will become your new hobby. And that is the second reason for trying new things: to have some innocent fun.

Trying new things means learning. Opening your mind to the world you did not know about. Opening your horizons. You will wake up the part of your mind that is curious and eager and open to experimenting and risking.

Trying new things also means the opportunity to meet new people. People who are interested in the same things. They can become new friends or possibly even something more in time. And you will definitively not have any time to be alone or lonely.

Have parties

Now that you are alone, especially if you do not have kids or the kids have flown the nest, you can enjoy your home in any way you want. Including having parties. You might want to start by inviting your closest girlfriends. Watch some rom-coms together over wine and snacks, play games, watch old videos from college, or just talk and laugh.

Once you realize how much you enjoy having your friends over, you will start thinking of more elaborate parties. Cook up a storm, try your favorite recipes, and invite all the people you enjoy.

If you do have kids, let them have parties with their friends. Lay down some basic rules and let them have fun. They are also going through the adjustment period now that their dad is not living with them, so they should enjoy some of the benefits the situation brings.

Invited on a date? Go for it

You might not feel up to dating just yet and the person who invited you might not be as attractive as you would like. But it means the opportunity to get out, have a conversation and get to know a new person. Who knows, you might end up with a new friend, someone who likes the same books or enjoys hiking. It does not have to be a romantic attraction. Slow down with that.

Try to enjoy your job

If you have a job, it is something that will get you out of the house and among your colleagues and possibly friends. If you like your job, great, enjoy it. If it is just a way of making a living, try to see it as something more. See if you can find some fun in it, do it a little better by taking some courses, or finding a better way to do it.

If you are a teacher, try to make your classes more fun for your students. If you are an admin assistant, try to be as efficient as possible, learn a new app or redecorate the office. It might not be the right time to think about a new job or new career, but you can make your current job more fun. It is amazing how much you can do if only you put your mind to it.

Enjoy your house

Roaming through the empty house only brings memories of good times you had in it with your ex. It is likely that some of his things are still around. Everything reminds you of him. You feel like it is not your home. So make it your home. Redecorate, declutter, paint walls, buy new furniture or at least some new sofa covers and bed sheets. Bring in some flowers, potted plants, candles, and fluffy curtains. All those things you could not do before because your ex did not like them.

Chapter 10

Get out

Getting out will force you to stop ruminating about your divorce and just how alone you are. Well, if you go to the gym, you will not be alone. You will also do so much good for your health and probably for the way you look. And let's not forget those endorphins.

If you like hiking or walking outdoors, you will also get the benefit of fresh air. There is something about nature that makes us humble and aware that we are a part of something big and majestic.

Get a dog

If you have a dog, you already know how much your dog is helping you get through your divorce. You can talk to a dog; he never answers back and is never judgmental. Dogs offer an unlimited quantity of love. You can use it. Dogs also force you to get out; they need it but you need it too. Being outside will force you to see the change of seasons, the phase of the moon, and the clothes people wear. You will recognize your neighbors, maybe have a chat or get invited to a party.

If you think you are too busy for a dog and think it would not be fair to the dog to leave him alone in the house while you are working, think about how that dog feels in his cage at the animal shelter. In your home, he has you to wait for and love and look forward to you coming back.

Develop new routines

We are such creatures of habit. Most of our lives consist of routines that are well-established and make our lives more comfortable and predictable. Divorce destroys all those routines.

How to be happy after a divorce

You are in a habit to continue doing the same things you used to do while married, but doing them can be a painful reminder of your past life and the fact that you are now doing it all alone.

But, changing your routines can be hard. It requires a conscious effort. You are probably not ready for such effort while still in the first phase of grieving for your marriage. But, at some point, you will realize that it is necessary to cut ties with the past so that you can build the future. Developing new routines can fasten this process if you deliberately make new routines that are fun and pleasant and will make you not miss the old ones.

Make a fancy cappuccino in the morning instead of your normal black coffee before you rush out of the door. Get up earlier to do your self-care routine, the new routine you should start your new life with. Make pancakes or strawberry smoothies or chocolate chip cookies for breakfast instead of boring oatmeal. Have weekly lunch with the kids, or your besties if you do not have kids, in your favorite restaurant. Once a week, go to work in the community garden or soup kitchen. Cook dinner with your kids and teach them to make their favorite dishes. Read them bedtime stories even if they are teenagers, just choose some age-appropriate stories.

Get an idea? New routines that are fun will soon become the symbol of your new improved life. Loneliness? A thing of the past.

Give your garden some love

If you have a garden, you probably used a gardener in your married life. You cannot afford a gardener anymore and in any case, you should spend more time in the garden and get your fingers in the dirt.

Gardening is so beneficial that psychiatrists even recommend it to dementia patients. It is a combination of physical effort (digging, weeding, chopping, cropping, carrying things around), growing something from seeds, picking up fruits of your own labor, watching the whole process of growth, and enjoying the pure beauty of the flowers, trees, and bushes.

It is not uncommon to get into an almost Zen state while gardening, lost to the outside world. Do it even if you have just a small balcony or a patch of neglected soil in your front yard. Create a paradise where there is nothing now. Symbolic or your new life, right? You will be alone while gardening but being alone will be a pleasure.

Declutter your life

Decluttering is something we normally associate with clearing the house of excess stuff. We have excess stuff in all aspects of our lives and decluttering will give you a sense of purging old, unnecessary, and stressful things out and opening space for yourself to breathe. Space in your home, in your closet, in the kitchen cabinets, but also in your wallet. Get rid of most of your credit cards. Get rid of membership to clubs you do not want to belong to anymore because they remind you of your previous life.

Most importantly, learn to declutter your mind. After divorce, you will be sitting alone on your grand sofa in your grand living room, ruminating over your past, feeling sorry for its loss. For the loss of all that you thought was possible.

Get rid of those thoughts that are unproductive, that cannot change anything and only make you sad. Replace them with new dreams and hopes. Every time you start thinking of the past things you used to do with your ex, push the thoughts aside and think of something you want to do and now you can.

Build your self-reliance

The fear of the future in which you will have to take care of everything all alone is a common fear after divorce. You are not used to it; for so many things, you relied on your husband.

You probably did not learn where the breaker box is or how to change oil in the car or how to replace a washer in the faucet. Learning to do all those things will give you great sense of empowerment and confidence.

You have to tell yourself that now you can rely only on yourself and that you can and will do it. It does not mean that you literally have to do everything alone. You have neighbors, family, and the phone to find tradespeople to fix things. You are in control. Instead of crying about having to do things alone, be proud of your self-reliance. Even if you have to learn how to change the darn oil in the car on your own.

Chapter 11

Designing Your Post-divorce Life

How are you doing? Getting better? Ready to move on? Let's find out together.

Prerequisites for moving on:

1. You can talk to your ex without anger and resentment. This will be your first sign that you are moving from the state of grief for the loss of your marriage and all dreams you had together, to being ready for the new phase of your life.

   This is especially important if you have children. Your ex is not capable of hurting you anymore, he has done that but now does not have that power anymore. But he can still hurt your children if they believe that he does not love them anymore or that they are somehow at fault for the divorce.
   It is crucial for your peace of mind and the future of your children that you and your ex can work together on parenting your children. If you can spend time in the same room without having your anger rise and wanting to punch him, you are on the right track. Work on that.

2. You have a circle of people you can lean on, who were there for you through all the post-divorce stages. They are loving and supportive, non-judgmental but not afraid to tell you to cut it out when you go on a self-destructive runt or feel self-pity.

   That circle of people you trust with your life, and who you love so much that you would move mountains for them, are your tribe, your rock, the support system you can count on for the rest of your life. They proved it.

3. Your kids are adjusted to the new reality. They feel happy again, there is no anger towards their father or taking sides about whose fault the divorce is. Their lives are in balance again, they have a loving relationship with their father and they see him regularly.
4. Your finances are in order. You got a decent child support or alimony, or you have your job or pension. You have some savings for emergencies.

Sorted out all that? Did you also have some time to take care of yourself?

1. You established your self-care routine.
2. You re-examined who you are as a person now that you are not a part of a couple.
3. You fortified your resilience and self-confidence and feel strong enough to deal with just about anything. You actually did.

Tired? Exhausted from the emotional roller-coaster and enormous changes? Totally normal. Spend some time pampering yourself. Do nice things for yourself only. Meet your besties for lunch and some laughs. Go to a spa. Buy a new dress. Go to a museum. Rest. Do nothing. Meditate (similar to doing nothing but with the purpose of emptying your mind of endless ruminating).

Now what?

At some point, you will start thinking about the whole rest of your life. You are not so despondent anymore and you have a more positive outlook now that you've established that you are strong and resilient. You feel that you are ready for that future you promised yourself. But what do you really want?

Write down the description of the life you always wanted. Be specific: you wanted to be a painter/singer/dancer/teacher/zookeeper. You always wanted to live in Costa Rica. You wanted to live a simple life in a cabin in the woods.

Write down your wildest dreams. Do not think about only realistic dreams or things you believe are possible. Include everything. It is your list. You can dream as much as you wish. Play with that list for a while. Do not show it to anyone just yet or you will get a lot of dream-crushers under the guise of realism and practicality.

What is possible?

There are two important obstacles to fulfilling your wildest dreams: kids and finances. If your kids are still small, you have to postpone really wild dreams like moving to an ashram in Tibet, or you have to include them in that dreams. They do have kids in Tibet.

Finances are much less of a big obstacle than many will let you believe. First, we need much less money to be happy than we are led to believe in our consumer society. Second, you can always work, now that Covid showed us how many jobs can be done from home, wherever that home is.

Let's examine all possibilities and just how realistic some enormous changes you are dreaming about are.

Quitting your job

If you hate your job, you cannot have a happy future. Working for money and for paying bills is soul-crushing. Just look at the people around you. Is there something you know you would be good at and that you can turn into a job? Do some research.

Many jobs can be done from home. Everything that you can do using your computer can be done from home.

You might want to talk to a head-hunter, or browse through job sites or freelancing sites to get some idea of today's job market.

Evaluate honestly what your skills are. You might have skills you do not think of as something that can make you income. You are a good seamstress? Good designer? Writer? Editor? Illustrator? Interior decorator? Woodworker? Many things that you did as a hobby, things that you love, can be turned into a profession.

Selling your house

You might have been forced to sell your family home as part of the divorce proceedings. Look at it as a blessing in disguise. You do not want to be reminded of your unhappy past all the time. You do not need all that space anyway. Why spend time cleaning it when there are so many better things to do with your time?

Think about how and where you would like to live. Moving close to where you work would mean no commute. Walking to work means exercise, getting to know your neighborhood, and not having to own and maintain a car (another huge expense). No commute means so much more time for fun things such as stopping for a cocktail after work or going to a yoga studio on the way back home.

Think carefully about how you really want to live. In a modern high-rise, with a clean, Zen interior? In a quaint cottage with a little rose garden? In a historic house you can restore lovingly over time? All that is possible now.

Moving to another country

This is much easier if you do not have children or they are in college or grown up. There must be countries and places you visited and loved. Go back there and look once more; this time, thinking about living there long term. It is a different thing from visiting as a tourist. Can you deal with cultural differences? Language? Lack of basic services? Poor medical care? Can you find a job? Can you find housing you can enjoy? Is there an expat community that you can join and get help from?

If you have kids, moving them with you will depend first on whether their father supports your plans. If not, that idea is out until they are adults.

If your ex is supportive, you have to think about their schooling. Are there schools that they will fit in and which will provide them with the education that is adequate to prepare them for college? You also have to convince them that it is a good plan and what is in it for them. Just learning another language and having experience in another country will be a huge advantage once they start looking for a college or a job.

You do not need to work for a living?

If you got a decent alimony, you are ready to retire and have a pension, made a decent investment and have enough interest you can live on modestly, or your grandma left you her house, or you have a trust fund, you most likely have enough money that you do not have to work for a living.

Does not look like a lot of money? In this new phase of your life, you have to seriously evaluate your priorities. Do you really want to continue living the same lifestyle you had as a married woman? Did it make you happy? Are you willing to keep doing your hated job to maintain it? Think about it carefully.

How much money do you really need to live comfortably? Talk to your gardener/maid/poor relative and ask them how much money they live on. Look for a friend who 'quit it all' and moved to a farm in the bush to paint or write. Ask him or her how much money they spend every month. You might be shocked at how little we need to fulfill our basic needs.

This is where the de-cluttering we discussed before comes in. Once you start de-cluttering your life, you will find out that there are so many things that are not making you happy. There is a de-cluttering rule that you should only keep things that make you happy. If you take this rule seriously, you might end up with your Kindle and your dog.

We are talking about our compulsive shopping and accumulating material things. This is where most of our money goes. Things do not what make us happy for longer than a day or two. It is people and experiences. Think about that.

There are two very important things you can do if you do not have to work for a living: volunteering and going back to school.

Think about volunteering

Volunteering can be a perfect combination of getting a new job in the field you enjoy, doing something useful with your life that benefits others and moving to another country. There are agencies that employ experts who are willing to spend a year or more in a developing country where their expertise is needed. Some of them require you to fund your volunteering on your own. If you can afford it, great. Life in developing countries is usually cheap and does not require a big investment.

There are also agencies that cover your expenses such as rent and food during your volunteering. You will need your money only for luxuries such as traveling to neighboring countries or having cocktails with your colleagues when taking a break.

The expertise needed in developing countries ranges from doctors, engineers, and computer programmers to teachers, nurses, and gardeners. Teaching kids English is in great demand and you can certainly do that!

One thing about volunteering on this scale is that it will radically change your life. Many of your values will be put into perspective. You will learn about who you are and what you are good at. You will learn a lot. And the satisfaction of being able to change the lives of hundreds of people cannot be measured.

Going back to school

Going back to school can change your life in so many ways. The question is: are you ready for it? Did you get married after college and never practiced your profession? Now is the time to go back to that. Many things changed since you last studied and you have to boost your knowledge. Look for a master program you would enjoy, or which would allow you to look for a more interesting job.

If you never went to university, there is never a better time than now. It does not matter how old you are. There are courses specially designed for seniors. There are online courses you can do from your home.

It is also great fun going to a class full of kids the age of your grandchildren. You will enjoy it more than you can dream. Kids are so full of enthusiasm and joy. It is contagious. Going on a field trip with them and climbing some cliffs to see that endangered bird might be challenging, but oh so much fun.

If you are not looking for a new job, you can study just about anything: from comparative philosophy and art history to growing bonsai. Why not quantum mechanics? You do not even have to do exams if you do not want to.

What matters is that you are learning something new, something you were always curious about. And do not forget all the science about how learning keeps dementia at bay and keeps you young long into your old age.

Are you getting excited? Eager to start? Scared witless? All normal. The possibilities are endless. If you are not ready, you are not ready. If just thinking about those enormous changes makes you appreciate what you have, that is great.

Do serious research about any of the big changes you are contemplating. The Internet is a great source of information. Get in touch with people who are already doing what you are contemplating. They probably have their website or a Facebook account. It will not be difficult to find them.

Once you make your decision, at least a preliminary decision, it is time to relay it to your support team. Prepare answers to all possible questions they will have. Keep in mind that you do not have to follow their advice, but it is good to have it. You need their support in this new, exciting adventure. And once you make up your mind, after seriously evaluating pros and cons, they will support you. They really want to visit you in Tibet or Costa Rica.

Chapter 12

Love Again

Are you wondering why this chapter is all the way at the end? There is a very good reason for it. Did you enjoy divorce? Of course not. Nobody does. It is a nightmare. But jumping into a relationship and/or marriage soon after divorce means that your next divorce is just around the corner.

OK, so you do not want a divorce, but you do want love. Love is everything that makes life worth living. Don't put love and marriage in the same bag. They are very different, not necessarily linked or related.

One of the worst consequences of divorce is the all too common feeling that you lost love and that nobody will ever love you again. Or that you will never find anyone worth loving again.

You are allowed to think that at the first throes of grief over your marriage collapse, but soon after the strongest emotions are gone, you will realize that it is rubbish.

It was only one man that does not love you anymore and who you do not love anymore. There are a few billion of them left out there. So, are you going to start looking for the 'right one' now? There are a few things you need to sort out first.

Never again

There is a lot you have to learn from your divorce and one of the most important things is not to get into the same situation again. How?

Love yourself

Divorce probably did a number on your self-confidence and sense of self-worth. You are probably not even sure who you are. Most likely, the marriage did a pretty good job of making you feel unimportant, unlovable, boring, and frumpy. You were too busy taking care of your husband, kids and home to think about yourself. Well, now is the time to change that.

It is not all about looks. It is about your sense of self. We discussed it in previous chapters and how to boost your self-confidence. You need to convince yourself that you are worth loving and you need to start by loving yourself.

If you do not love yourself, it will be pretty apparent to anyone else who comes into your life. The more self-love you feel, the more you can attract people and situations that promote your well-being.

So what do you do now? Go for a makeover? It is not about the looks.

When you love yourself, you accept yourself the way you are, your weaknesses, faults and strengths. You do not have to make excuses for your mistakes or shortcomings. You have as much compassion for yourself as you do for others. You have a strong sense of your values and purpose.

There is one easy way to learn how to love yourself: do for yourself what you would do for anyone else you love. If a friend or your daughter came and asked you: How can I love myself? What would you tell them?

- *Practice being mindful.* Be aware of what you feel, think, and want. Being mindful means you know who you are and you act on this knowledge. You do not care what others think of you or want for you.

- *Be aware of the difference between needing and wanting.* If you can ignore or turn away from something that is exciting and attractive and focus on what makes you centered, balanced and strong. When you stay focused on your needs instead of your wants, you are able to ignore automatic patterns of behavior that brought you nothing but trouble in the past.
- *Make self-care a priority.* Take good care of all your basic needs. You love yourself when you nourish yourself every day through healthy habits—good nutrition, regular exercise, enough sleep, and a healthy social life.
- *Set boundaries* for yourself. Set limits to too much of anything—work, love, or harmful, energy-depleting activities—that does not reflect who you are.
- *Protect yourself.* Keep only the right people in your life. Stay away from those who secretly enjoy your loss and pain instead of your success and happiness. Life is too short to waste on them. You will respect and love yourself more.
- *Forgive yourself.* It is normal to take responsibility for our actions, but it is not the reason to punish yourself forever for mistakes you made while growing and learning. Accept that you are human and not perfect. Only then you can really love yourself. Try to be less hard on yourself every time you make a mistake. Remind yourself that experiences you can learn from are not a failure, just lessons learned.
- *Live intentionally.* Live with design and purpose, even if your purpose is not completely clear to you. What matters is that you intend to live a meaningful life. Your intentions will help you make good decisions and feel good about yourself. When you accomplish what you set out to do, you will love yourself for it.

Love others

Love comes in all shapes and forms. We need love in our lives, but you can find it very fulfilling to express love to your parents, friends, children, or colleagues. You can love nature, the garden, your dog, and your home. Show them that you care, and do small things of kindness and love for them. Fill yourself with love.

Practice empathy. Try to see what other people feel and think before judging them for their behavior. It will help you to forgive.

Do not look for love

It is tempting to get into a steaming relationship right after divorce to show yourself that 'you've still got it.' It is never satisfying for any amount of time. As long as you know who you are and love yourself, that someone special will appear in your life.

Be yourself. Be the best version of yourself, but do not go doing makeovers or plastic surgeries in order to attract that someone special. If he needs you to have a boob job to be perfect for him, he is not perfect for you. There is someone out there who is dreaming of meeting a woman like you. Open yourself up to experiences and you will have a chance of meeting him without looking for him.

Look for companionship

When you are looking for love, you are probably subconsciously or consciously looking for someone who will eventually become husband no. 2. Why? There are so many interesting phases between the first and second marriage if marriage is what you are seeking.

Start by finding a companion. Maybe more than one. Someone whose company you enjoy, who you will get to know and do things with that you both enjoy. If you do not focus on him being 'the one,' you will enjoy the companionship without pressure and expectations. And who knows, before you know it, the two of you might decide that you are just what both of you were looking for to start the next phase, the marriage.

Go on dates

Feel free to go on dates, lunches, parties, picnics, and outings. Meet people, flirt (you need practice after years of marriage). Have fun. If you find someone interesting, get to know him better. Learn what he likes and dislikes. Go for long walks and talk about ideas, philosophies, values, and interests. See if you are compatible. After your first marriage, you know just how important compatibility is. Unless that is what you want, make it clear to your date that you are looking for companionship, friendship, and fun and not just quick physical contact. You will find out from your friends that dating in the 21st century is complicated and better avoid any misunderstandings.

Explore different hobbies

We discussed it before: do something you like, new or old. That is the best way to meet people you will find interesting and who will find you interesting. Do not be afraid of doing something new you are not good at. That is a great opportunity to accept the helping hand of someone nice.

Sari's story

There is a famous waterfall in Jamaica that tourists and locals love to walk through, uphill all the way. Sari was enjoying climbing through fast-running water, over slippery rocks, laughing when falling into the water and getting wet. While her friends looked for the easiest ways to go up, Sari went to the most challenging parts. It was really hard but, fortunately, there was always a strappy, young local man willing to offer a hand and support.

After they got to the top of the waterfall, friends asked Sari why she was choosing such a challenging part of the waterfall. She replied: "I was not trying to prove how strong and skilled I was. I just wanted to have some fun. Which of us had more fun? I had help all along and I even have a date tonight."

What are you looking for?

It is crucial that after the divorce you think long and hard, totally honestly, about what went wrong. Not whose fault it was, but what was really wrong with your marriage. It will get clearer once the strongest emotions are over and you can think more rationally. Did you have fights over money? Religion? Parents? Was one of you jealous? Did you respect each other? Did you like the same things? Did you have the same values? For example, did he occasionally say little white lies he did not consider important and which drove you crazy? What about politics? Did you fight over political candidates and their policies?

Think about what the most important issues were. Things you absolutely would not accept any more. This will pretty much give you a clear picture of the kind of person you are looking for as your future partner. Do not make compromises over important things or turn the blind eye to things you do not like just to please the new person in your life. It is a sure path towards the same pattern that ended your first marriage.

Go slowly

Say you are lucky enough to meet a person you really like, you click on so many levels, you spend every available time together, and eventually you decide you would like to share a home. If there are no kids, your consideration is whether to give up your current apartment.

What if it does not work out? Take it slowly, cautiously, and carefully at the beginning. If you are an impulsive type and you can afford it, convince him to move in with you. That way, you can kick him out if it does not work out. Sounds cynical but look at all those romantic movies. Someone is always moving out; it better not be you.

Marriage is not necessary

Marriage is a legal contract. It is not a romantic notion. It is designed by society, church and government to legalize finances, children's welfare, and property. Maybe sex. Not much more. It is not necessary to get married to a person you love just so you can put it on your Facebook profile. Marriage is expensive and divorce is even more expensive.

Think long and hard about whether getting married is really necessary. The first time, it was a part of every girl's dream: white dress, big ceremony, all the drama and romance. The second time, that is not the necessary part. So if you want to get married, you better be sure it is what you want and need.

Conclusion

You made it to the end! How do you feel? Tired and emotionally drained, or ready to start this new, exciting phase of your life? Probably a bit of both.

Getting through a divorce and coming to the point when you feel like you are ready to enjoy life and make necessary changes to make this new life the best one possible is a process. No reason to rush. Enjoy the process by being aware of what you are consciously doing, on your own, intentionally, planned carefully and capable of implementing. It is all you.

By now you know that you do not have to be perfect in order to be happy. That you are great just the way you are, but if you want to be the best version of yourself, there are so many ways to make it happen. You learned how to boost your resilience and self-confidence so that you are better equipped to deal with any future difficulties life will throw at you. You learned to love yourself, faults and all, so that others can love you too.

We discussed the importance of learning from your divorce. Why it happened, not whose fault it was. As they say, "It takes two to tango." What really matters to you and things you absolutely refuse to compromise on. It is so easy to turn a blind eye to some very important issues in order to avoid confrontation or to please the new man in your life, once you come to that. If you want him to give you the respect and love you deserve, you have to learn to love and respect yourself.

We also discussed the power of being alone. Of the peace and freedom being alone offers. Even if you have never lived alone and cannot imagine living life without a man in it, give yourself a chance to experience living alone. It is well worth it.

Conclusion

One of the most important things you gained with your divorce is the freedom, and the opportunity, to redesign your life. We discussed all the ways you can direct your life after divorce. The change is already here, so you might as well make it the change you always wanted. You might prefer to make small changes such as rearranging furniture or painting walls, moving to a new house, getting a new hairdo, or going all the way: going back to school, getting a career you always wanted, moving to a different country or devoting your life to doing good for others.

Do not be afraid of love. To love and be loved. You are capable of both. Maybe you're not ready yet, but just let it happen by being open to the possibility and opening your horizons, taking chances, trying new things and meeting new people.

Do you feel the power now? The hope, but also the challenge? It is a wonderful feeling to grab the reins of your life in your own hands and feel the wind in your hair. Divorce was hard, but it is now behind you. And the whole bright future is ahead of you.

Bonus Material

Letting Go Affirmations

You will agree that after divorce, you can use any help you can get to pull out of the dark pit. Affirmations are powerful little tools that do wonders, cost nothing, are easy to use and you can shape them and use them in any way that works for you. You can even come up with new ones. If they work, share them with others.

What are affirmations?

How you think and talk to yourself when you are in a crisis of confidence such as divorce matters very much. You might not even be aware that you are not treating yourself nicely. You are calling yourself names such as 'naïve idiot,' 'stupid, gullible girl,' 'hopeless loser,' and the list goes on.

You would never allow anyone to call you any of those names, but you feel free to use such names for yourself. In a way, it is worse. You need to intentionally change this negative path and start moving towards more positive thinking. Here is where affirmations come in.

Affirmations are short phrases that you need to repeat regularly in order to shift your negative thought patterns, motivate yourself to make positive changes and boost your self-esteem. You can also call them your 'daily mantra.'

If you think of affirmations as a New Age construct, you would be wrong. There is solid research behind the usefulness of affirmations and how they actually work.

Affirmations have been found to affect the brain's processing and reward system. Scientists discovered that research participants who regularly used positive affirmations that reflect their values had more intense activity in their brain's reward center. Their brain's neural processes linked to the positive self-view and self-competence were more active than the participants who didn't use self-affirmations. In short, their brain was rewarding them for using affirmations by making them feel good about themselves.

How to use 'letting go affirmations'

You must have heard or seen on the internet affirmations that resonated with you. There are affirmations for any difficult situation you might go through. They all have a particular purpose. When you are coping with the aftermath of your divorce, your purpose is to begin healing, to reestablish a sense of security, to restore your trust in humanity and to regain your self-confidence.

Affirmations work best if they are repeated regularly until what you are saying sinks in and you really start believing it. To develop the new custom, create a new little ritual for yourself: write all 'letting go' affirmations you like on individual cards or pieces of paper. Put them in a pretty box or jar and pick one up every morning before having to face the world. Read it out loud. Let it boost your armor and your confidence when facing whatever the world throws at you, including your ex.

Here is a list of some of the most popular 'letting go affirmations' to choose from. You can find many others, so feel free to add them to your collection.

- All my feelings are normal.
- Beyond my divorce, there is a new adventure for me.
- Change is difficult, but it will make me stronger.
- Change is natural, even difficult ones, but I can handle it.

- Day by day, bit by bit, I am getting stronger and more powerful.
- Divorce is just a new beginning.
- Each day takes me closer to my new, better life.
- Everything is going to work out just fine.
- I accept all of my emotions.
- I let only kind and well-meaning people in my life.
- I am ready for pleasure and sensuality in my life.
- I always do my best.
- I am a good person.
- I am a lovable person.
- I am a positive person.
- I am a unique person, and I will deal with this in my own way.
- I am complete just as I am.
- I am working on becoming the best person I can be.
- I am compassionate and kind toward myself.
- I am capable and strong.
- I am building a better life for myself.
- I am enough.
- I have enough.
- I am exactly where I am supposed to be.
- I am filled with the spirit of healing and calmness.
- I am full of joy and happiness.
- I am grateful for everything good in my life right now.
- I am grateful.
- I am grateful for being me.
- I am well-grounded.

- I am healing bit by bit every day.
- I live in the present; I do not dwell on the past.
- I am growing every day.
- I am learning so much through this experience.
- I am worthy of love.
- I am able to love.
- I am becoming more aware of my strength as I am learning to be on my own.
- I am not a failure.
- I am a survivor.
- I can deal with all my fears.
- I am open to the beauty of the universe.
- I feel safe and secure.
- I am strong.
- I am supported.
- I am in control of my own life.
- I am grateful for everything I have learned in marriage.
- I am happy to be me.
- I believe in myself.
- I am able to find the good in this situation.
- I refuse to carry grudges against anyone.
- I opt for kindness for myself and for others.
- I choose to have a hopeful and positive attitude.
- I connect with other people without losing the sense of who I am.
- I deserve to be happy.
- I deserve to be respected.
- I deserve to be safe and secure.

- I don't know how this divorce will get sorted out, and that's OK.
- I am not looking for perfection, just improvement.
- I expect great things in my future.
- I experience and release my emotions in a healthy way.
- I feel my own strength.
- I forgive myself and others who hurt me.
- I live in peace and overcome bitterness and anger.
- I have much to be thankful for.
- I have a great future ahead of me.
- I have all I need.
- I have the courage to dream of a better future.
- I know what I need and want.
- I am letting go of a painful path to follow a different, new one.
- I love myself exactly as I am right now.
- I respect myself.
- I rise above fear.
- I rise above feelings of shame and guilt.
- I take things one day at a time.
- I trust in my body's ability to heal.
- I trust in myself.
- I trust in others.
- I trust my intuition.
- I trust myself now more than ever.
- I trust the way life unfolds.
- I accept that some things are out of my control.
- I will be happy again despite everything.

- I will become stronger than ever through this divorce.
- I will change my life for the better.
- I will handle this change with grace and calmness.
- I will hold on to hope.
- It takes courage to go through a divorce; I have great courage.
- My best times are coming.
- My courage is unlimited.
- My heart is tender and wounded; I will protect it and heal it with kindness.
- My life is changing, and that is OK.
- My life is full of grace and beauty.
- My life is getting better and better.
- My potential is endless.
- My thoughts are focused and clear.
- Nothing can overwhelm me.
- One day soon, my life will go on and the divorce will be a thing of the past.
- Pain is normal, it will pass and I will emerge whole and happy.
- There are happy days ahead.
- There is laughter and joy in my future.
- There is no difficulty I cannot handle.
- These difficult times will bring me a happy, new future.
- These troubles are temporary.
- This divorce is just an episode in my life.
- Time is bringing healing and peace.
- Today, I am rebuilding my life.
- When I feel sad or angry, I accept and move on.
- I can do this.

How to be happy after a divorce

- I will be just fine.
- I am strong and resilient; nothing can crush me.
- There is nothing wrong with me.
- I will not let divorce define me.

References

A Non-linear Look at the Stages of Grief. (2022). *Hospice and Palliative Care of Chenango County*. Retrieved from https://hospicechenango.org/a-non-linear-look-at-the-stages-of-grief/?gclid=Cj0KCQiAwJWdBhCYARIsAJc4idAM0jxXXRdGws_r1GgwpqoIQSYcmzyjKo51W-WV94DAqET6FEyyZ1QaApyXEALw_wcB

Brower, E. (2020). Your Brilliant Life After Divorce. *Gabriela Hartley Esq. Divorce Law and Mediation*. Retrieved from https://gabriellehartley.com/your-brilliant-life-after-divorce/

Coping With Separation And Divorce. *Mental Health America*. Retrieved from https://www.mhanational.org/separation-and-divorce

Cuncic, A. (2022). What Is the Holmes and Rahe Stress Scale? *Verywell Mind*. Retrieved from https://www.verywellmind.com/what-is-the-holmes-and-rahe-stress-scale-6455916

Divorce Can Feel Devastating, But It's Not the End — 12 Tips to Start Anew. *HEALTHLINE*. Retrieved from https://www.healthline.com/health/life-after-divorce

Dworkin-McDaniel, N. (207). Life After Divorce: 12 Ways to Rebuild Your Life. *Everyday Health*. Retrieved from https://www.everydayhealth.com/emotional-health/life-after-divorce-12-ways-rebuild-your-life/

Epton, T., Harris P.R., Kane, R., van Koningsbruggen, G.M., Sheeran, P. (2015). The impact of self-affirmation on health-behavior change: a meta-analysis. *Health Psychology*. Retrieved from https://pubmed.ncbi.nlm.nih.gov/25133846/

Frey, M. (2022). The Truth About Why a Breakup Can Cause Weight Loss. *Verywellfit*. Retrieved from https://www.verywellfit.com/the-truth-about-break-up-weight-loss-3495398

Goldman, R (2022). Affirmations: What They Are, Health Benefits, and Getting Started. Everyday Health. Retrieved from https://www.everydayhealth.com/emotional-health/what-are-affirmations/

Hald, G.M., Sander, S. & Strizzi, J.M. (2020). Anxiety, depression and associated factors among recently divorced individuals. *Journal of Mental Health*. Volume 31, 2022 - Issue 4. Retrieved from https://www.tandfonline.com/doi/abs/10.1080/09638237.2020.1755022

Hines, S. (2017). How to cope with divorce, from women who've been there. Good Housekeeping. Retrieved from https://www.goodhousekeeping.com/uk/news/a568703/how-to-cope-with-divorce-tips/

How to Overcome the 6 Hardest Things About Life After Divorce. *SAS for Women*. Retrieved from https://sasforwomen.com/how-to-overcome-the-6-hardest-things-about-life-after-divorce/

Kelly, J. B. (2000). Children's adjustment in conflicted marriage and divorce: A decade review of research. *Journal of the American Academy of Child & Adolescent Psychiatry, 39*(8), 963-973. Retrieved from https://pubmed.ncbi.nlm.nih.gov/10939225/

Nielsen, L. (2014). Shared physical custody: Summary of 40 studies on outcomes for children. *Journal of Divorce & Remarriage, 55*(8), 613–635. Retrieved from https://doi.org/10.1080/10502556.2014.965578

Pilosoph J. (2013). Being Alone After Divorce: Why It's Okay and Tips on How to Enjoy It. *Huffpost.* Retrieved from https://www.huffpost.com/entry/being-alone-after-divorce_b_3560504

Schwartz, B. (2022). The Effects of Divorce on Children & How to Help them Cope. *Choosing Therapy.* Retrieved from. https://www.choosingtherapy.com/divorce-and-children/

Teachman J. (206).Body weight, marital status, and changes in marital status. *Journal of Family Issues.* 37(1):74-96. Retrieved from https://www.ncbi.nlm.nih.gov/pmc/articles/PMC4714799/

The Top 5 Most Stressful Life Events and How to Handle Them. (2015). *University Hospitals.* Retrieved from https://www.uhhospitals.org/blog/articles/2015/07/the-top-5-most-stressful-life-events

Vos, P. Thomas, M.E., Cisneros-Franco, J.M. &Villers-Sidani, E. (2017). Dynamic Brains and the Changing Rules of Neuroplasticity: Implications for Learning and Recovery. *Frontiers of Psychology.* Retrieved from https://doi.org/10.3389/fpsyg.2017.01657

Thank you

Thank you for choosing to read this book. I hope that it resonated with you and gave you the courage and a few tricks and tips to go through such a traumatic experience as divorce. I hope you will use the book to remind you that, regardless of how painful, this phase of your life will pass and you will emerge on the other side wiser and stronger for the experience. If you enjoyed the book and found it useful, please take some time to leave a review. It would be appreciated not only by the author but by so many other women who are going through the same traumatic experience as you.

Printed in Great Britain
by Amazon